PAISLEY GOES WITH NOTHING

DOUBLEDAY
NEW YORK LONDON TORONTO
SYDNEY AUCKLAND

PAISLEY GOES WITH NOTHING

A MAN'S GUIDE TO LOOKING BETTER, FEELING BETTER, AND FOR ONCE BEHAVING AS IF YOUR HEAD WASN'T SEWN ON BACKWARDS

HAL RUBENSTEIN
WITH JIM MULLEN

A MAIN STREET BOOK
PUBLISHED BY DOUBLEDAY
a division of Bantam Doubleday Dell Publishing Group, Inc.
1540 Broadway, New York, New York 10036

MAIN STREET BOOKS, DOUBLEDAY, and the portrayal of a
building with a tree are trademarks of Doubleday,
a division of Bantam Doubleday Dell Publishing Group, Inc.
Portions of this book have previously appeared in a different
form in the *New York Times Magazine* and *Interview*.
Paisley Goes with Nothing was originally published in hardcover by
Doubleday in 1995. The Main Street Books edition is published by
arrangement with Doubleday.

Book design by Gretchen Achilles

The Library of Congress has cataloged the
Doubleday edition as follows:
Rubenstein, Hal.
Paisley goes with nothing : a man's guide to style / Hal Rubenstein
with Jim Mullen. — 1st ed.
p.   cm.
1. Men's clothing.   2. Grooming for men.   I. Mullen, Jim (Jim R.)
II. Title.
TT617.R83   1995
646'.32—dc20   95-1238
                                                    CIP
ISBN: 978-0-385-48393-3

144915995

FOR MY MOM—

WHATEVER THE REST OF YOU HAVE,

WHATEVER THE REST OF YOU BOUGHT,

WHATEVER THE REST OF YOU OWN,

WHATEVER THE REST OF YOU KNOW,

I HAVE HER, SO I WIN.

ACKNOWLEDGMENTS

To pass yourself off as a know-it-all, you have to ask a lot of questions and know whom to ask them of. I thank these people for being there when I needed them, when I didn't know I needed them, and for listening patiently when they had other things to do:

Swami Asokananda, Lisa Bankoff, Lisa Baum, Tim Buckley, Gene Chace, Garth Condit, Gina Davis, Tony Dean, Carrie Donovan, Janet Froelich, Gai Gherardi, Laurel Graeber, Nick Graham, Jami Morse von Heidegger, Donna Karan, Calvin Klein, Larry Hotz, Brendan Lemon, Steve Lischin, Aggie Markowitz, Barbara McReynolds, Barry Miguel, Thom Oatman, Dr. Jay A. Okin, Joan Oliver, Claudia Payne, Debra Rubenstein, Howard Rubenstein, Keith Scott, Linda Silver, Ingrid Sischy, Dr. Howard D. Sobel, Florence Macy Stickney.

CONTENTS

SECTION 3
TAKE TIME

SECTION 4
BEHAVE

WHY MEN NEED THIS BOOK

Okay, fella, we'll make this quick because it's obvious you're a little uncomfortable picking up this book and probably wouldn't be if the check-out line were moving faster.

So, what do you know?

Probably what most men do.

How many miles you get to the gallon, who's to blame for your team's crummy season, exactly what you'd do if you ran the company, in which carton are your electric trains.

That's it. We've come to the end of your road.

That's not enough.

Men should know how to buy a suit, how to cook without a barbecue, how to make a bedroom not look like a dorm, what excuses a woman won't accept, how to show a client a good time, when it's time to say good night, how to pick out eyeglasses, and who goes first through the revolving door.

You're not supposed to get stymied over what to wear to an interview, stupefied when it's time to pack, stumped as to what Mom might want for her birthday, and rendered senseless should anyone say you look sexy.

Yet:

◆ You won't send food back.

◆ You can't commit to a color unless it comes with antilock brakes.

- Shopping's your nightmare.

- Taste is what Mom said.

- Responsibility is what Dad said.

- Common knowledge is what friends think.

- Style is something everyone else seems to have more of.

- And charm is too exhausting to sustain.

Face it, buddy. You don't know how to live.

But it's not your fault.

There's a good reason why she dresses to look beautiful, while you dress not to make a mistake.

You were never taught any different.

What did Dad show you besides how to throw a ball, step into a pitch, and prepare for a lay-up shot? How to tie a tie (one way), how to tie your shoes, and the way to ask for a regular man's haircut—"not too much off the top."

Did he ever say to you, "You know, son, it's such a nice day. Let's go shopping"? Or, "Why don't we go to the market and pick up some fresh fruit?" Or, "How about we find a nice Merlot and shoot the breeze?" Didn't think so. And now you're hungry, and you're thirsty, and you've got really boring stuff to wear.

Imagine if Dad had never taught you how to play basketball and you wanted to learn now. How would you do it? You couldn't ask your friends. They'd laugh their butts off. You could hire someone to teach you by the hour, but then you'd spend a fortune renting a court, because you wouldn't dare let anyone see you. Most likely, you'd never learn. You'd buy floor seats for every Knicks game and yell like a jock on Methedrine.

Well, you're not alone. It's what happens to most men when it comes to style. You're never taught how. And people dislike doing anything they're not good at. That's why you haven't a clue as to what flowers women like and what lingerie they don't, where to press to determine a melon's ripeness or how to tell if the shoe fits.

The result is, you and your comrades wander aimlessly through malls, supermarkets, and first dates looking as if you'd just driven 80 miles for a Grateful Dead concert without noting that your tickets were for tomorrow night.

You can't go on this way. All right, you can. But why? The problem is that to find some solutions, you know you'll have to do the one thing you hate doing more than standing outside the fitting room in Better Dresses.

Ask for help.

(If you happen to be a woman reading this, and are having a hard time relating, remember the last time you were lost and a half hour late but your male companion, who was driving, stubbornly passed by four gas stations in a row speeding down another road to nowhere? If you can imagine what's it like to do that every day, then you have an inkling what it is to be a grown man.)

Well, it's your lucky browse, fella. Just seconds before the millennium, this book is offering you salvation.

In a society where work and play always mix, where

books are judged by their cover, where *you* are judged by the company you keep, and rightly so, *Paisley Goes with Nothing* takes as its inspiration the advice of the big mama on the D train who picked up her pocketbook and swatted her two unruly children upside their heads while offering some better-listen-to-this advice: "I only have two words for you, 'Be have!' "

Life's a lot more fun once you learn how.

Just think. Within your grasp is a world where Christmas presents can be better, sheets are all cotton, food is ready when company comes, the wrong things don't always pop out of your mouth, it's not so hard to "match," and everyone saves time at the revolving door.

Style is fun. It sure beats what you're doing now.

And all you've got to do is admit, "I don't know."

And then want to.

A CONCISE CRASH COURSE IN DAILY LIFE

5 THINGS MEN SHOULD NEVER GO OUT SMELLING LIKE

Any aftershave meant to evoke where the wolf first saw Little Red Riding Hood

Patchouli oil

The five cartons of cigarettes everyone around you smoked last night

Anything medicinal, hygienic, or cosmetic that's mentholated (no, you're not provoking images of a cool mountain stream; you're reminding people of clothes they've still left in storage)

Anyone whose keys you don't have

7 THINGS YOU DON'T EVER WANT TO BUY AT THE LAST MINUTE

Cuff links

A needle and thread

Deodorant

An umbrella

Tickets to the sellout you said you'd get tickets to

Orchids

A swimsuit

bathing suit

5 FLOWERS YOU DON'T SEND TO ANYONE YOU CARE ABOUT

Carnations

Gladioli

Dyed daisies

Heliconias and birds of paradise, unless your intended loves discos

5 THINGS PEOPLE DON'T DO ANYMORE

Polish their shoes

Pull out a chair for a woman, or anyone for that matter

Look you in the eye when shaking your hand at a party

RSVP on time

Remember that a man doesn't shake a woman's hand unless and until she extends hers

10 THINGS PEOPLE SHOULDN'T DO ANYMORE

Talk on a cellular phone in a restaurant

Trust their doctor to have all
the answers

Assume cigarette butts aren't
litter

Let their VCR continue
blinking 12:00

Dress in black just because
they're going to a revitalized
neighborhood rechristened
with an acronym

Pack a suede jacket when
traveling to any location
damper than Phoenix

Think black tie always means
a tuxedo

Try to raise ficus trees in
their apartments

Wash their hair every day if
it's on the dry side

Pretend that love is all you
need

13 THINGS YOU SHOULD TRY ONCE

Boudin

Walt Disney World

Getting to a party exactly on
time (you'll never hurry
again)

Reading Jane Austen

Going to the movies alone

Wearing a piece of jewelry
(wedding bands and school
rings don't count) without
thinking everyone is looking
at it

Taking a long, honest look in
the mirror

Yoga

Going a whole day without
eating meat or dairy products

Wearing a fabric you've always thought of as luxurious

The opera and a hockey game, preferably during the same week

Sending a thank-you note the next day

Volunteering

16 NUMBERS YOU SHOULD COMMIT TO MEMORY

Your shirt, waist, collar, sleeve, inseam, shoe, suit, and ring sizes—and the equivalent data of anyone you buy gifts for

The octane minimum for your car

How many feet in a meter

The one on the stub for the coat you just checked

Your average monthly total in bills

The cab you get into

The date of your parents' anniversary

How much is in your checking account before you go to Rhinebeck, Las Vegas, or Saks

The total cost of a leased car, not the amount of its monthly payment

6 WAYS YOU GET JUDGED UNFAIRLY

Your car

Your luggage

Whether or not you eat red meat

Your cologne

The way you throw

Your job

You know what L.S./M.F.T. stands for.

They talk *Star Trek* and you drop William Shatner.

5 CLUES YOU MAY BE WITH THE WRONG AGE GROUP

Your clothes have creases.

All your laces and strings are tied.

No one knows who Marlo Thomas is.

6 HINTS YOU'RE IN THE WRONG STORE

The lighting was inspired by *Tommy.*

You've been wandering for five minutes and no one has yet said "Can I help you?" or at least "Good afternoon."

The staff dress as if they could veto your promotion and behave as if they'd seen you on *Hard Copy.*

The salesperson tells you you're hard to fit.

You can't recognize any tracks on the tape.

You got spritzed twice on the same floor.

Three-way mirrors.

You don't suffer a five-minute penalty for paying cash.

The staff recognize you the next time you're there.

8 SIGNS YOU'RE IN THE RIGHT STORE

You're not afraid to touch the displays.

The salespeople are wearing clothes they like, perhaps have even bought.

They ask what you already have in your closet.

They knock before they open the door to your dressing room.

They don't tell you you look good—they show you why you do, or don't.

11 WAYS TO LOOK YOUNGER THAT DON'T COME IN A TUBE

Drink lots more water.

Get more sleep.

Meditate.

"Eliminate coffee & cigarettes"

Eliminate coffee and cigarettes.

Be regular.

Get out of debt.

Make time for friends.

Change your attitude.

Sand your elbows.

Stretch.

Laugh.

5 INDICATIONS YOUR CLOTHES FIT

No one tickles an exposed piece of skin right when you are reaching farthest.

You can hug yourself indecently.

You almost smiled when you caught yourself in the mirror

(and then the doubt patrol showed up).

You don't readjust every time you stand up.

You can dance in them.

Indication that your clothes fit:

You can dance in them.

6 WAYS TO EDIT YOUR WARDROBE

Do it with someone else— preferably younger whom you neither sleep nor golf with.

Look for dry cleaning tags from laundries that have closed.

Admit that if you didn't wear it all last season, you never will.

Admit that if you haven't lost the weight in a year, you probably won't fit into it again while it's still in style.

You saw something you have on someone else—and it was a revelation.

Let your kids pick out five items apiece for charity.

5 HINTS YOU'RE WEARING TOO MUCH BLACK

You approach your closet with a flashlight.

You sense your local priest is jealous.

It takes more than 10 minutes for your date to find you in a crowd.

Gray is starting to look colorful.

Widows tell you to cheer up.

4 SIGNS THAT A SHOE IS NOT—OR TOO MUCH—FUN

The sole is as high as the heel.

It has more perforations than your colander.

No animal would recognize the skin as one of its own.

The salesman keeps referring to how comfortable they are.

5 NECESSITIES YOU CAN NEVER FIND THAT START WITH THE LETTER *S*

Scissors

Studs

Shoehorns

Shoelaces

Saran Wrap

4 CONSTRUCTIVE APPROACHES TO THINNING HAIR

Baseball caps (why do you think they're suddenly so popular with those over 35—team spirit?)

Wearing it short

Acknowledging that shoulder-length fringe is more Ben Franklin than cool

Reading Maria Riva on Yul Brynner

8 ELEMENTS TO SUCCESSFUL ENTERTAINING

A corkscrew

An '82 Bordeaux

Candles

Garlic

A deck of cards

An umbrella you can lend

Your wishing they would leave

12 THINGS TO KNOW BEFORE THEY ARRIVE

That garlic, olive oil, lemon, and whipped cream can fix almost anything

That you can figure 10 people per bottle of liquor, 4 for wine

A bathrobe softer than terry cloth

An extra Interplak attachment

6 THINGS GUESTS SHOULD NEVER SEE AT A DINNER PARTY

That everything you need to purchase, except ice, should be bought by the day before

That someone perky will come early

You, not ready

Liver

Bouillabaisse

The sink

Paper dinner napkins

That your medicine chest will be inspected

That everyone will help clean, except for the last course

That guests' manners are in

inverse proportion to the number of people who show up (even if they're your friends)

The phone number of a car service should anyone get real jolly

6 WAYS TO HIDE THINGS THAT ARE TOO LATE TO FIX

Ice cream

A hat

A turtleneck

Throw pillows on the floor and say you've just returned from Morocco

A garrison belt

A trunkload of flowers

5 REMARKS PEOPLE WILL THANK YOU FOR MAKING

About the something green on their teeth

"Half-mast, buddy!"

Where to vote

What color brings out their eyes

That they're dragging a yard of toilet paper

4 REMARKS NO ONE WILL THANK YOU FOR MAKING

"I used to go out with her too."

"Gosh, you look tired."

"I think you missed the litter basket."

That wearing that red ribbon doesn't mean you're actually doing anything about it.

In a restaurant during an early bird special

London

3 PLACES YOU SHOULD GO DRESSED TO DIE FOR

A great restaurant where you've made no reservations

Your mother's (it's about time she saw you looking good)

Wherever they're giving you the award

5 PLACES WHERE YOU'LL NEVER BE UNDERDRESSED

Upstate

Sitting in economy

Nightclubs in a strip mall

7 REALITIES YOU FORGOT ABOUT SUMMER

Tying drawstring pants makes love handles look worse.

Living with wrinkles.

Eating at least two hours before swimming—not because of what Mom said, but so your stomach doesn't look bloated.

Never letting them see you sweat is like trying to clog-dance through a dune.

The way salt water makes your hair very creative.

Fantasizing way too much.

So, that's why you do squats!

5 PLACES NOT NEARLY AS MUCH FUN AS THEY SOUND

Atlantic City

The Cannes Film Festival

The Honeymoon Suite

Backstage

Alumni Day

7 NECESSITIES MASQUERADING AS LUXURIES

A tuxedo

A massage

A vacation, just the two of you

Dinner at a restaurant scoring higher than 27 in the Zagat guide

Cotton sheets

A second language

Psychotherapy

4 SURE SIGNS THAT THE SHOPPING CART BLOCKING THE AISLE BELONGS TO A MAN

Who else buys one roll of toilet paper?

The ice cream and frozen dinners are on the bottom.

There's the meat. Where're the vegetables?

Every package says EXTRA, CHUNKY, or NEW.

6 DRINKS WORTH MAKING WELL

A classic martini

Something fruity and stupid

A chilled glass of champagne

A Coke float

A vanilla milkshake

Black coffee

10 MUSTS TO HAVE IN THE CAR

A detailed map covering a 50-mile radius from your house.

Tissues and napkins.

Windex.

Breath freshener and eyedrops.

A valet key (which starts the car but will not open the trunk).

Quarters.

A tape of the *1812 Overture* or something eye-openingly similar.

For wee-hours driving only: Need to stay awake? Nix the No Doz. Buy a pint of rock-hard high-butterfat-content ice cream (it melts more slowly). Place it snugly between your legs. Your nuts will freeze, but at least you'll get home with both of them.

11 WAYS YOU'RE JUDGED WITH GOOD REASON

Your politics (better have some)

The way you dance

How you treat a waiter

Your shoes

Bathtub ring?

If you know the difference between *Francis Albert Sinatra & Antonio Carlos Jobim* and *Sinatra's Duets*

How you carry money

What happens after two drinks

What you do to your voice when you talk to children

Your taste in chocolate

Your friends

5 APOLOGY ALTERNATIVES TO FLOWERS

A tape containing the five best *Mary Tyler Moore Show*s (Chuckles the Clown; Veal Prince Orloff; Phyllis learns of Sue Ann and Lars's affair; Lou, Murray, and Ted daydream about life with Mary; Lou and Mary date) and the last *Newhart*

An invitation to come over and watch *Two for the Road*

Bath salts (much sexier, and safer, than perfume)

Letting yourself be seduced in a part of the house without a mattress

Paron's dark-chocolate-covered popcorn

8 ACTIONS YOU SHOULD KNOW HOW TO DO

Tie a bow tie on someone else

Cook a meal from scratch in someone else's kitchen

Keep a secret

Swim

Hondle at a flea market

Console someone without platitudes

Change a diaper

Let yourself be seduced in a part of the house without a mattress

5 REQUESTS THAT EXPLAIN MORE THAN ANYTHING ON ANY QUESTIONNAIRE

"List your five favorite films—off the top of your head." (Not best, favorite.)

"Where and what was the best meal you ever ate?"

"What's the last CD you bought?"

"What's your idea of a perfect day?"

"Tell me about your family."

6 OBSERVATIONS THAT REVEAL MORE THAN "WHAT'S YOUR SIGN?"

How one eats

What's in the trunk of the car

The sheets on the bed

The shampoo in the shower

The CD that's put on when you come over for the first time (if you're asked what kind of music you like, say, "Anything")

Underwear, if any

underwear

30,000 REASONS FOR WEARING HIKING BOOTS WITH A SUIT

Potholes

6 SHAKY RATIONALES

"Look, it says 'No Fat' on the label."

"Three long hairs are better than none."

"It's not my fault they're homeless."

"I only smoke when I drink."

"I have big bones."

"I'm combining business with pleasure."

5 REASONS WOMEN LAUGH AT MEN

Because they still think everything should match.

Because they look at a menu for five minutes and then ask, "What should I have?"

Because you didn't win—your team did.

Because Steven Seagal is a jerk.

Because men don't laugh at themselves.

6 TENETS OF GOOD DINNER CONVERSATION

Don't be afraid of silence.

If you can't help it, start with a margarita.

Stuck? Talk about what's in front of you. At least, that's one experience you're sharing.

Read the paper that day. Or at least watch *Entertainment Tonight.*

Learn to accept a compliment with grace. It helps if there's something stuck between your teeth when you smile and say thank you.

Don't bring up *The Celestine Prophecy.*

7 ACTS YOU DON'T PERFORM IN A RESTAURANT

Breaking up.

Laying your keys on the table.

Loosening your belt and

exclaiming, "I don't know about you, but I'm stuffed." Pretty.

Lying to the waiter that everything is okay when it's not. Think whom you're really inconveniencing. Now think about who's paying.

Smoking while others at your table are eating, even if the management allows it.

Snapping your fingers for attention, unless you are headlining the floor show in a Spanish restaurant, and wearing one of those great dresses with the train and all those ruffles.

Getting up to go to the cash machine after the check has been presented.

5 REASONS I'D RATHER SWALLOW RAW TRIPE THAN EAT IN PUBLIC WITH YOU AGAIN

You start before everyone else is served.

You don't look the waiter in the eye when ordering, and then grab the busboy by the arm and speak to him in broken English.

You tip by doubling the tax exactly, regardless of the quality of service.

You dine in a three-star restaurant and all you can talk about is business.

You gesture with silverware.

YOU MUST REMEMBER THESE

If you're one in a million, there are 5,000 people just like you.

Your personal trainer is seeing someone else.

Nature abhors a vacuum cleaner.

Whoever's waiting on you only has two speeds, and you won't like the other one.

Reverse psychology still takes you in the same direction.

They don't make moviegoers like they used to.

It's last-minute shopping only if you plan to die later in the day.

50,000,000 Frenchmen *have* been wrong—at least twice.

If you dress well, people think you have a personal life.

SECTION 1

COMMON SENSE

THINGS EVERY MAN MUST HAVE

1. A fog-free shaving mirror

2. A black silk knit tie

3. Tiffany note cards on the heaviest stock

4. A black wool crepe suit—the first thing to pack on a business trip

5. Good wineglasses

6. Black cowboy boots with sloped heels

7. Nose hair tweezers

8. Something cashmere

9. A sewing kit that doesn't come from a hotel bathroom

10. Two sets of all-cotton no-iron sheets

11. At least one Randy Crawford album

12. A hairbrush not made of New Age plastic

13. *Halliwell's Film Guide,* no earlier than the sixth edi-tion

14. A bottle of good champagne in the fridge

15. A black bathing suit

16. A great leather belt with a sterling silver buckle

17. Something your father gave you

18. Black jeans

19. A Rowenta steamer—the second thing that gets packed

20. Julia Child's *The Way to Cook*

21. White jeans

22. A leather jacket, any style, as long as it makes you feel so cool you can hardly stand it

23. An up-to-date passport

24. A moisturizer designed specifically for the face

25. Two Ennio Morricone soundtracks

26. A white shirt so fine it doesn't need a tie or jacket

27. A suede brush

28. Scotch tape (for lint)

29. A bedroom with no mementos from college days

30. A topcoat that comes below the knees

31. A real madder tie

32. Silk pajamas (don't knock 'em if you haven't tried 'em)

33. Two tickets to a championship game, at least once a year, your choice

34. A way of seeing the sides and the back of your head so you can tell if you've covered the bald spot

35. Two black turtlenecks of different weight

36. Condoms

37. A dictionary too big to fit in a briefcase

38. A bud vase

Scotch Tape for Lint

39. A pair of Ray·Ban aviator glasses

40. A skin-care regimen that includes scruffing, a mask, and a night cream, but doesn't include deodorant soap

41. Long silk underwear (nothing is warmer—ask friends who ski)

42. An outfit too sexy to wear in public

43. Enough underwear and socks to go two weeks without laundering

44. Lobster crackers

45. A full-size umbrella that wasn't bought on the street

46. Collar stays besides the ones that came with the shirt

47. A Burberry Vyella shirt

48. A subscription to *Consumer Reports*

49. Gift wrapping that isn't for Christmas

50. A copy of your favorite childhood movie

THINGS EVERY MAN MUST HAVE

1. How to write a thank-you note

2. The birthday or anniversary of anyone whose picture sits on your desk or rests in your wallet

3. A good tailor and magical reweaver

4. That nothing will make you feel better before you get off a plane than putting on a fresh pair of socks

5. How to tie a full Windsor knot

6. One clean joke

7. The difference between worsted, crepe, and twill

8. How to give a compliment

9. How to take a compliment

10. The private number of at least three wonderful restaurants and the first names of their respective maître d's

11. That you don't put salt around a margarita

12. One card trick

13. The colors you can't wear and the suit cuts you can

14. The Zen of washing dishes

15. The names of two uncommon champagnes—and that you don't open either by making the cork pop

16. That if you can go a whole season without wearing a particular piece of clothing, you should give it to charity

17. One poem by heart

18. How to cook at least one good meal

19. The European equivalents of your sizes

20. Your mate's important sizes

21. That you're supposed to go through a revolving door before she does, so you can push

22. That sewing is not woman's work

23. How to play poker

24. The way to find the North Star

25. The names of a dozen different flowers (mums don't count) and of a florist who'll deliver them

26. That you never read the newspaper or eat anything while wearing suede

27. CPR

28. That the only woman who will ever love you unconditionally is your mother

29. How to make friends with a three-year-old

30. Where you vote

31. When it's your little brain talking, not your big brain

32. That Philip Roth, and not Norman Mailer, is the conscience of his generation

33. How to shine a pair of shoes without ending up like you're auditioning for a minstrel show

34. The name of whoever does your dry cleaning

35. That strong-arming, calling out to, or snapping for a waiter is only slightly more attractive than chewing with your mouth open

36. That it doesn't matter how good your recent workouts have been if you haven't done abdominals

37. The shape of your face

38. Kiehl's Rare Earth Facial Cleansing Mask stops razor cuts faster and less painfully than a styptic pencil

39. You put neither cinnamon nor chocolate atop a cappuccino, and "espresso" is pronounced as it's spelled

40. An unconstructed jacket should not be cheaper just because it doesn't have a lining

41. That when a woman says no, she means no

42. Camcorders are to spontaneity what a hailstorm is to the U.S. Open

43. That you never show up for dinner at anyone's house empty-handed

44. That unless your hair is incredibly oily, you shouldn't wash it every day

45. That if you spill red wine on the carpet, spill white wine on top of it immediately

46. Someone who gets you into a showroom sale

47. When to leave

48. Saying "I don't know" is not as unattractive as you think

49. That your father understands you better than you think

50. Good taste is not nearly as much fun as style

WAYS TO PUT IT ALL TOGETHER BETTER THAN THE WAY YOU USUALLY DO

73

1. Your socks should never be funnier than you are.

2. Unless you don't have much to draw in, avoid drawstring pants.

3. A belt fits correctly when the buckle's prong goes through the strap's third hole.

4. A high-waisted person should avoid high-waisted pants, unless it satisfies his Eddie Haskell fixation.

5. Maybe you wouldn't appear so uncomfortable in the afternoon if you bought your own underwear and knew your own size.

6. Never wear a plaid jacket to a job interview.

7. The only effective way to wash out petroleum-base pomade is with soap.

8. There is no regulation width or length for ties. So knot one before you buy one.

9. Wash, shave, gel, polish, and—use your head, genius—brush your teeth *before* you put on anything more than underwear, or do you enjoy invoking the name of St. Jude while you try to get MFP fluoride off your tie.

10. Iron, John.

11. The best shoes to dance in are sneakers with no tread left.

12. Clothes don't make you look fat. Fat makes you look fat.

13. If you are tired of apologizing for your had-to-work-late-no-time-to-go-home-and-change corporate look, leave one black and one cream-colored turtle- or crew-neck sweater in a bottom desk or file cabinet drawer.

14. Must you always carry every key you own?

15. Better you should always carry a *usable* handkerchief.

16. If you know you are going to need them handy, carry your business cards in your *outside* breast pocket.

17. Does your mother come in to clean five times a week? Then hang up your clothes.

18. Your underwear shoudn't be briefer than your favorite bathing suit. Sooner or later you're bound to be seen in both.

19. Do you love the scent of your deodorant more than life itself? Then don't buy polyester active wear or workout clothes.

20. Paisley goes with nothing.

21. You're not supposed to smell your own cologne once it's on.

22. Don't waste money on any if you smoke.

23. There's no such thing as classy luggage if you have to lug it.

24. Don't iron the stuff you get from mail-order catalogues.

25. NEVER press jeans. (If there are creases in yours, wear them in private, among close friends, until they fade.)

26. Clothing makes an excellent sunscreen.

27. What's the point of a short raincoat?

28. Threadbare old favorites saved "to knock around in" are never knocked around in. There are plenty of charities more than happy to put them into action.

29. Old ski lift tickets are not a fashion accessory.

30. If you don't have muscles, don't wear muscle T's.

31. Don't wear an ascot unless you've been there.

32. When it's below freezing, close your coat. We're not impressed.

33. Silk shirts are much warmer than they look. If you sweat like a showerhead, don't wear them on the big presentation day, out dancing, or on a first date.

34. Turning up the collar on a knit shirt is appropriate only when imitating Katharine Hepburn. If it's about a nasty hickey, resort to either a turtleneck or a devilish grin.

35. There's nothing wrong with a man buying a fur coat, as long as he's giving it to someone who goes to a gynecologist.

36. If you're over 5′ 5″, and can remember how you felt when Monroe died, don't ever wear overalls again.

37. Unless the corona from a total eclipse is coming through the skylight, take the sunglasses off indoors.

38. Get your hair cut a week before the big day.

39. Literally tuck yourself into a bathing suit. These things don't take care of themselves.

40. A belt *and* suspenders?

41. If you wear boots often, try a boot wallet.

42. If you think a blue blazer goes everywhere, think twice before you go anywhere.

43. If you must have a blue blazer, and you must, buy the best one you can afford.

44. What a shame you weren't born with a family crest. Well, pray for one in your next life, and live without one in this.

45. Thin, wiry shoelaces need to be double-knotted.

46. To remove the old hem mark from a let-down pair of pants, soak the line in white vinegar and then iron with a warm iron.

47. A reminder for those who insist on going bare-ankled, even in the hottest and steamiest of climates—you can always throw the sweatiest of socks into the wash, but loafers tend to give it up in the spin cycle.

48. Pinky rings look so cool if you're in a Martin Scorsese film.

49. Beware of showroom and final clearance sales-fever reasoning, i.e., "Hey, for $20 . . ." Once clothing is in your closet, what you paid for it is forgotten. How it looks is all that matters.

50. If you must have your clothes monogrammed, do it where it can't be seen.

51. Tweeze your nose hairs; the ones inside—and the ones on top.

52. If you're over 40, your ears now need a haircut too.

53. When the invitation says "black tie," how come she opts for a dress that she keeps lovingly wrapped in tissue, while you rent a been-to-the-dry-cleaners-more-times-than-Vikki-Carr's-sung-"It Must Be Him" dinner jacket? Be a grown-up. Buy one for your very own.

54. Massages relax you, and the more relaxed you are, the better you look in your clothes.

55. White jeans are not out of season in winter. White leather shoes are not in season, ever.

56. The only time you're not better off shopping alone is when buying eyeglass frames.

57. A little flannel goes a long way.

58. Despite their prevalence, button-down oxfords worn under double-breasted jackets are more the Fred and Ethel than the Lucy and Ricky of fashion.

59. More people look better in solid navy than they do in solid black.

60. Don't pull loose threads. Cut them.

61. Jewelry on the beach can be very attractive. It certainly is to sharks. They like shiny things.

62. Buy shoes in the late afternoon.

63. "You have to break them in" is an old wives' tale. Shoes should feel good before you hand over the charge card.

64. Men should use a moisturizer as often as women; in other words, every time you wash your face.

65. Loosening or taking off your tie does not make you look sporty. It makes you look drunk.

66. When confronted by a person wearing reflective aviators, look him square in the eye, and then start fixing your hair.

67. If you like something so much, buy two of them. You may not come across it again.

68. Safari jackets look pretentious when you're on one, and too far out of Africa when you're not.

69. Don't hang up sweaters, not even cardigans, or the lady of the house will soon belt them and wear them with leggings.

70. There's a time and place for everything, except dickies.

71. Don't regard your wardrobe as a series of outfits.

72. Getting dressed is supposed to be fun. Try to have some.

73. No wire hangers, ever.

Your socks should never be funnier than you are.

SECTION 2

SPEND MONEY

YOU'VE GOT A LOT OF NERVE—

ABOUT EVERYTHING ELSE

MAKING CHANGE

Men who beg off change used to be decisive, and very generic. "You're not going to get me in that. No way." But within recent years, the disinclination has gotten much more personalized, and far more tentative. Now the retreaters are more likely to start with "It's not that I don't like it. It's just that . . ."—and then they choose from a wide selection:

1. "I'm too old";

2. "I'm too short";

3. "I have no place to wear it";

4. "I can't wear that to work";

5. "My wife'd kill me";

6. "My kids would laugh at me";

7. "I'd feel funny";

PLUS my favorites:

8. "It's not my style";

and the existentially classic

9. "I don't know."

(Combinations are allowed.)

Well, it's a step. At least it shows there are a lot of noses pressed up against the display glass, and that men are aware that others of their sex are deserting the battalions of cowards if only because they're tired of the uniforms. The problem is, diverse as they may seem, these excuses are weaker than Tom Watson's putting or the Mets' starting lineup.

1. *Too old* compared to what? Whom do you think these clothes are made for? Kids? The models who wear them? They can't afford them. Maybe you can't either, but no designer who wants a bigger palazzo in Sardinia is going to focus all his attention on either a generation that can turn a sweatshirt, a kerchief, and a pair of cutoffs into fashion, or an idealized image. You're falling for the media. What you have to do is fall into the Gap and a few dozen other stores. What you see in magazines, on TV, and from runways is theater. To thrive, current menswear has to be far more adaptable than you give it credit for. To thrive, so do you.

2. *Short*, tall, squat, thin, knock-kneed, round-shouldered, barrel-chested—what else? Defects are everywhere. And if they were sufficient reason to ban men from wearing current trends, designers wouldn't be allowed to don their own clothes. Okay, a short man in a frock coat looks like a walking toaster cover, and a tall man in overalls should have on big shoes and a red nose. You can't wear everything. But what do you have on now? How come that's okay? How different do you think the clothes hanging on store racks with sleeves and buttons and collars are? Try something on for once. You'd be surprised.

3. & 4. You get dressed, don't you? You go to dinner, don't you? The theater, movies, away on vacation? So, what's the problem? *You have places to go.* That's what clothes are meant for. No one's insisting you dress like Heathcliff or that tying one sweater scarflike round your neck, with two others plopped over your head and one more wrapped skirtlike round your waist, is the only way to fly (though what a great way to pack for a weekend).

There are new forms and textures worth learning about, most of them comfortable, flattering, sexy. Yet you haven't been paying attention, so how could you know that suits have become the most adaptable and essential clothing base, outside as well as inside the office? If you're still wearing the same old stuff to work, you can bet that, unless you're the boss, when you walk in the conference room, you're making as big an impression as you would giving a Masai warrior a copy of *Martha Stewart Living.* You don't have to be that different. A little different will do.

5. Blame *the other one*. Is there anything lamer? Especially since your partner would probably burst from joy.

6. *Your kids* are walking around with everything four sizes too large and nothing tied, rags on their head, and shoes way too big for their feet, and you're worried about them laughing at you? They're babies, but babies who've found what works for them. It makes them feel cool, vibrant, alive. Maybe you should find something that does the same for you.

7. What did a golf club feel like first time you swung it? Working with a computer initially, when you touched the keyboard? Moving in with someone you loved? *Feeling funny* is good. We should feel funny more often.

8. All right. Let's explain this once and for all. *Style is not fashion*. Clothes don't have style. You have style. Yes, you. You just may not know it. Because, guaranteed, you exhibit style in other areas. You just haven't trained it on getting dressed. For *true style is the quality of imagination*. It's the ability to place yourself in new situations with a fresh attitude and an eye on something better. You don't think you have that? Then what to wear is the least of your problems.

9. *You don't know?* Who does? Some people just guess more confidently than others. As Jane Wagner once wrote for Lily Tomlin, "Reality is a collective hunch." Try sticking your two cents in. It's how you make change.

THE MATCH GAME

YOU'RE TRYING TOO HARD

Lucky you. One-button jackets are back. Oh, and so are ones with two buttons, three buttons, four, five, as well as double-breasted ones with six, eight, and 10 buttons. They're showing suitings with wide lapels, narrow ones, and no ones, as unencumbered as cardigans alongside the revived silhouette that includes shoulder pads. Some of the coolest ties out are almost four inches wide, but there are plenty just-as-nice ones that are barely two inches across. Have you seen all those shirt collar shapes? And pant legs are so wide, except when they're so narrow. But that's because you can't rely on merely one width to look as good with work shoes as with sandals, or cowboy boots, or brogues, or those new high-cut English lace-ups. Most interesting of all is that if things around town progress as they usually do—big firms setting precedent for smaller ones—pretty soon your company may not care which combination of these items you select to wear to work. Isn't that great?

Bet you're thrilled.

As if casual Fridays and "creative black tie" weren't bad enough. All sure bets are off. The rules could soon be yours to make. Though never much of a fashion plate, playwright Arthur Miller probably foresaw your current state of mind when he wrote, "Where choice begins, Paradise ends, innocence ends, for what is Paradise but the absence of any need to choose this action?"

Mr. Miller, however, never won a Tony Award for seeing the bright side. There's no reason to fret that picking a wardrobe that looks both fresh and modern yet right for work has to be a crucible. Oddly enough, despite all the possible variations, it's never been easier, provided you don't run off in a hundred directions at once.

All you have to do to start is follow one of the oldest tenets in clothing sales, a bylaw that any good salesman will offer you as a KISS. Now, don't get nervous. KISS is merely an acronym for "Keep it simple, stupid." The most dangerous path a man not used to shopping can follow is to turn over his whole wardrobe at once. There is no imperative to find the new you. The old one got you this far. Let's just clean him up a bit.

SUITS

Ignore all the choices for a moment—the shapes, the lengths, the colors—and concentrate on one flattering constant. Regardless of the suit you're curious about, the best look these days is fit, clean, and sleek. The wishful image promoted several years ago by showing up floppy and carefree as if you'd just wandered in off the beach is over. (Of course, for people with enough confidence and panache, no look is ever over, but we're talking about you.) What remains from that hard-to-relate-to concept, however, is an ease of construction in suit jackets that has now been transposed from baggy to leanly tailored, and it's currently available in all suit shapes. Consequently, though a jacket is once again more form-fitting, it need not be constricting.

Solid-color suits have never looked smarter or hipper. So stop knocking yourself out. If you wish to select something more intricate, keep the pattern small, the stripe simple and faint. Or choose a texturized weave or a twill with a subtle twisting to the yarn. Unless you're thin, shy away from checks and intricate computerized patterns. If you can't help yourself, however, and something blaringly elegant screams your name, keep your accessories as simple and basic as school uniforms.

MATCHING

Think about that KISS. Laying pattern upon pattern, stripe upon check, print upon plaid is complicated, risky and, more often than not, disappointing. Besides, it's a waste of time. You don't have to.

Nothing looks cooler than combining solids with solids. Dark colors with dark colors, earth tones with earth tones. Or wearing variations of the same tone. It's not necessary to match one navy blue exactly to another. As for matching lapel, collar, and tie widths, with rare exceptions, like follows like. Skinny lapel, skinny collar, thin tie, and vice versa. If you are like most men, who follow the edict of Yogi Berra, you know that if you think about it, you can't do it. Now you don't have to, so you can.

SHIRTS

The cleaner your choices, the better you look. But when all else fails, remember that white shirts are the *Cats* of accessories, because they are now and forever. As for collar variations, there are four kinds popularly available, but you're foolish to get yourself caught up in this multiple choice. The spread collar is fine for wide lapels and if you love big tie knots. Button-down shirts look geeky, uptight, and will make even the newest suit look slightly stale. Stick with a regular classic collar, which looks fine with almost every kind of suit. However, if you want to turn a knowing head, choose a collar with a slightly longer point, one that when worn with a four-in-hand knotted tie, will do the reverse of the button-down— the combination can make most suits look new.

TIES

Here is a mystery to outdo the Sphinx's. The average suit sells for at least 15 times the cost of a tie. It covers your whole body. It defines and shapes you. It's designed to say more about you than any other piece of clothing you have on. Then why do men, and their loved ones, feel obliged—worse, compelled—to upstage this presentation by buying a strip of silly, goofy, cutesy, critter-filled, career-indicating, carnival candy–colored fabric that screams "Look at this, and forget the rest"?

Listen up. The biggest compliment you can ever hope to get from wearing a yard of ostentatious silk is "Hey, snazzy tie." The biggest compliment you can get from wearing a beautifully cut suit is "Hey. Get a load of you. You look great." Which would you rather hear? A tie, by definition, is an accessory. Let it accessorize. Now, go pick one that will show off your suit and get out of the way.

SOCKS

Novelty socks look nasty and insincere. Under your pants is no place to hide a joke. Do you want women to suspect you have Disney characters frolicking on your bedsheets? A well-dressed man wears unobtrusive hose that act as a bridge between his shoes and his pants. Forget about pattern and concentrate on quality. Unfortunately, men don't ever think of buying socks, which is why they're always displayed near the check-out counter as a point-of-purchase item.

The most comfortable socks are cotton or a lightweight merino wool. When blended with about 20 percent nylon for shape and durability, they become even more practical. Cashmere socks sound great and feel luxurious, but cashmere was not meant to be pulled over heels and rubbed against ankles. They tend to fall apart after half a dozen launderings. Silk hose are great for skiing because they're so warm. They're also so sleazy. When wearing boot shoes, wear thicker socks to absorb the extra moisture from enclosed feet. Synthetic socks should not be worn by anyone with sweat glands.

Do more expensive socks last longer than cheaper ones? Not necessarily, but they feel better while they do. Look. Be grateful men don't have to deal with nylons and panty hose. The way women run through them, if men had to deal with the same thing, they might never get dressed at all.

S H O E S

Since the range of shoes and boots that can complement a suit is now so wide, it's more valuable to tell you which footwear doesn't look good:

Sneakers (not now, not ever, no exceptions, that's it, the end)

Espadrilles

Skinny classic Italian lace-ups that were once the epitome of sartorial taste

Weightless loafers that look like bedroom slippers

Wing tips with more perforations than a potato masher

Sandals with socks

The Frye boots you wore in college (buy new ones, cheapskate)

Thongs or Teva water sandals

Anything made out of plastic

Being barefoot (save shoelessness for those walks on the beach you no longer take in a suit)

Other than these, wear what you like. It may not be Paradise, but it's the best we can offer after the Fall.

TWO EASY PIECES

BUYING A SUIT

You'd probably rather mow the lawn, sit through your nephew's third-grade dance recital, or have your wisdom teeth extracted with an X-Acto knife. But unless you've developed technology from an episode of *Nova* the rest of us missed, a new suit is not going to find its way into your closet unescorted. You'd love to send somebody else out to get it, wouldn't you, the same way you acquire your underwear (that only half your shorts fit correctly is merely an unfortunate coincidence). Unfortunately, you have to go out and buy it yourself. So get moving. No whining that you don't know how. Learn. There's a new world out there. Try dressing as if you're part of it.

1. Rather than embarking on your usual aimless search for the usual Harris Tweed grail, before you start wandering through the racks, *decide what you are buying a suit for.*

◆ Business travel? Then the estimable qualities are weightlessness and the ability to lose wrinkles by simply being hung for ten minutes in a steamy bathroom. (Forget about the suit. Wouldn't *you* like to shake out that way?)

- Year-round usage? Remember that corduroy tends to retain beach sand.

- Determined to look more together on vacation than your kids think possible? Now, we're talking an unconstructed jacket with *at least* three buttons, and maybe a floppy pant leg that complements a sandal.

Knowing a suit's purpose in your wardrobe will narrow your field of vision and perhaps shorten your reenactment of the Diaspora in the men's department.

2.   *The more specific you can be about fabric, the better.* This doesn't mean you have to know the percentage of wool to silk in a blend. Common knowledge and common sense will do for openers. Traveling while on business? Then linen is out. Find low maintenance appealing? Then linen is out. Want your money's worth with a year-round garment? Then linen is out.

What you do need to know is that many wool blends dewrinkle quickly, wool crepe being the quickest and the most comfortable. Cotton weighs nothing. Corduroy makes your butt look bigger. Polyester, born again as microfiber, but with the Sybilline capacity to adopt personalities as varied as viscose and ramie, is now pliable, resilient, occasionally luxurious, no longer the flag bearer of cheesiness. Wash and wear, however, looks and remains as cheesy as it sounds.

Note: Linen *is* for remaining totally cool while looking fabulously careless. However, you can sustain the effect over long periods only if you never sit down. In fact, avoid leaning, reaching, and turning too quickly. Better yet, find a convenient wall, with flattering lighting, and don't move.

3.   You don't know what wool crepe or viscose is, do you? Don't worry. It's amazing how many guys reading this don't know what linen is. Nevertheless, whether you're swatch savvy or find even rudimentary classifications as cryptic as dialogue in a Frank Herbert novel, you must locate two things prior to shopping for a suit:

- ◆ At least one men's store that doesn't make you feel as if you're being judged as to whether or not you're worthy of its time.

- ◆ A salesperson in that store who likes his mission, does his homework and, most of all, listens. *A savvy salesperson is the most desirable accomplice to have in tow,* far more valuable than being accompanied by a male friend, which practically ensures purchasing either nothing or a duplicate of something you already own; or by a female one, which guarantees your dressing the way she sees you and permanently quashes any attempts at indulging in secret sartorial daydreams for fear of looking foolish in her eyes. As

for blood relations, shop with them when you're looking for a burial plot.

◆ *Try as hard as you can to go shopping alone. Tell the
others and yourself you're going out for the paper
and just keep walking.* If you're one of those fearful
of being sold a bill of no-goods, how come you've no
trouble tuning out an overly effusive car salesman's
blasting pitch, heading off a steamrolling real estate
agent, or disbelieving "Robbie," your waiter for the
evening, when he perkily proclaims, "Everything is
good!"? Regardless of your expertise in a particular
field, a snow job always sounds like a snow job. Relax, and pay attention. You'll know when you're learning something.

4.   *What do you want to spend?* Good-looking suits can be
found at all prices, but expect to pay at least $500 retail for a
suit that flatters you and offers enough quality to provide a
full-day's-wearing level of comfort. The technology is such
that it's become difficult to find a badly constructed suit. In
fact, there are now machines used in the manufacture of
"hand-tailored" suits that are actually programmed to drop
stitches. But constructed well and fitting well are not synony-
mous. Consequently, before you put up your price ceiling,
even if you have no intention of parting with this much of
your paycheck, *try on an expensive suit, especially if you
have never done so, if only to provide you with a frame of
reference as to what a suit should do for you,* what it can

look like on you, and what you ought to feel like in it. It's why a struggling law student test-drives a Porsche. It's the reason we have museums. You can't devise standards unless you know the range of possibilities. Is a taste of honey worse than none at all? Don't blame us.

5.   Great tailors—there are only a few left (the store that employs one boasts a major asset, though you won't know that for sure until after you buy at least one suit)—can work magic.

There are two areas, though, where their powers are of no use. *If a suit jacket does not fit in the shoulders*—if it puckers, drops too low, or is too restricting—*or if a jacket's too short or too long, TAKE IT OFF.* If you can't find the same one in a different size, too bad. Shoulders are to a jacket what a foundation is to a house. You tinker with shutters, not with a foundation. Pockets, lining, and line complicate toying with jacket length. (Remember, once they start cutting, you own it. For what you're paying, it's not worth the risk.) Besides, tailoring should be about altering fit, not design. Imagine yourself a tall man who slides behind the wheel of a Toyota MR2, to discover the top of your head smashed against the moon roof as the salesman tells you, "Relax! Loosen up! Slouch!" Do not compromise. Do not be persuaded.

6.   There is one less than obvious technical element you should be aware of—*the difference between a fused and an unfused jacket.* Between the fabric and the lining of the lapel, the shoulders, and the chest pieces is a layer of reinforcement. The engineering of this middle layer is an essential factor in determining price. Expensive garments utilize the insertion of one or more plies of either horsehair or regular canvas. There is not a machine yet made that can insert and secure this middle layer. An unfused jacket is always done by hand. More labor, more money. But because the horsehair or canvas remains free-floating, suspended by hand-stitching, it allows for more drape in the body, a soft roll to the lapel, more pliancy in movement.

The alternative process is called fusing, whereby a synthetic mesh canvas, treated with an adhesive, is permanently attached to the outer fabric by heat. When first developed in the '50s, fusing approximated the it-wears-you-military-appeal of Michael Rennie's immobilizing spacesuit in *The Day the Earth Stood Still.* Since then, life's gotten tougher, but fusing's gotten easier. Any suit lapel that exhibits a flat, no-nonsense appearance has been fused, but the graceful roll of a featherweight wool Dolce & Gabbana suit is also made possible by advances in fusing.

The hidden drawback to fusing is lurking not within, but without, the garment: poor-quality dry cleaners. Excessive heat or harsh chemicals can cause puckering and shrinkage. Either find yourself a good dry cleaner or make up the name of an obscure Belgian designer and tell friends you're wearing him exclusively.

7.   If any garment in menswear could sing out "I'm just a suit whose intentions are good. / Oh Lord, please don't let me be misunderstood," it would be the unconstructed jacket, or "This thing's got no lining," as most men refer to it. Ironically, because it's designed to be weightless as a big shirt and comfortable as an old cardigan, *in many ways the unconstructed jacket is the height of tailoring.* It can't rely on internal stabilizing factors, canvas backing, or any traditional ways a suit is made. All interior workings are now exposed and must be finished off, requiring more labor than if hidden by a lining. The drape and shape of the coat now rest on the inherent quality of the fabric (linen will waft appealingly, wool gabardine will hang like thinly sliced meat), the skill of the designer, and the sorcery of the tailor (though you will almost always find some reinforcement in the chest and shoulders). Want to know why an unconstructed jacket costs more than the others? This is why.

8.   *Looking at a suit*

- ◆ You never get more than you pay for.

- ◆ There should be no puckering or no bulk where the shoulder insets to the sleeve. If there is, it will not iron or steam out. If a salesperson promises you it will, ask to see another salesperson, permanently.

- ◆ If the desired fabric is plaid or stripes, look at the way the pattern is matched at the seams, how it is handled on the lapels, at the shoulders, and especially down the center seam in the back.

- ◆ A felt backing, not a backing of matching fabric on the underside of the lapels around the neck, is what you want.

◆ Look at the quality of the buttons—plastic, wood, horn—and how they're sewn on. If there is thread wound round and round between fabric and button, the buttons were probably sewn on by hand.

◆ Is the lining of comparable quality to that of the jacket? Is it fully sewn down? Is it sewn to the fabric at any point other than the edges, compromising movement?

◆ Flap pockets look best on business suits.

◆ All pockets and buttonholes should work.

◆ Look at the surgeon's cuffs. (Yes, my good man, that's what the area is called where the buttons are sewn on the sleeve, derived from times past when surgeons, usually dressed as befitting their pillar-of-the-community status, had to roll up their sleeves in emergencies and "operate.") Today, these buttons are more symbolic than functional, so it's not critical if the buttons don't work; but the evenness of their spacing (they should just touch each other) and of their finishing is an indication of craftsmanship.

◆ Are alterations included? Never assume.

9. *Looking at yourself in a suit*

◆ Because good-quality menswear, especially suits in

the upper price range, is about nuance and subtlety, you *must* try all garments on. Both parts. Stop thinking of this as such a hassle. Trying on suits is not a hassle. Chemotherapy is a hassle.

◆ When you go into a store, wear clothes that you can get out of easily—loose pants, slip-on shoes—and furnishings that form a blank canvas for what you're buying.

◆ Pick a suit shape that enhances your body type. Short and heavy? A low-slung double-breasted jacket will make you look like Sydney Greenstreet. If you insist on double-breastedness, choose a tailored, six-button silhouette. Big hips? A low, one-button closure breaks up the girth. Short jackets make your legs look longer. Center vents do not flatter ample rear ends. *The three-button jacket is the best all-around shape for all body types.* Short? Wear a high-button single-breasted in monochrome. Wide? Don't even smile at plaid, corduroy, nubbies, or cuffs. Tall and thin? Have a great time. It's not a fair world.

◆ Make sure the store you're in has a three-way mirror. You have to see yourself the way the world does, all 360 degrees. You wouldn't get up out of the barber's chair until he shows you the back of your head, would you? Well, you shouldn't.

◆ The back of the jacket collar should be flush with your neck. No dead space.

- Many men now know that you should be able to move freely in a jacket, but some go too far. There's no need to flap your arms about, unless you're too late to change for a sprint against Carl Lewis. Just bend, and reach, and see if anything pulls.

- The sleeve on a jacket should reach only to the fleshy part of the thumb. Any longer does not look hip. It looks studied and dowdy or as if you were still waiting for the director of the last version of *Lost Horizon* to yell, "Cut!"

- Suit pants should fit the same way as similarly cut dress pants sold separately. They are not supposed to be fuller because a jacket is covering them. Not everything Grandpa taught was true.

- Pants are sized by waist for a reason. It's astounding how many men wear their pants riding on their hips. If you're a Deadhead, and still into your old Landlubber jeans with the five-inch zipper, you're excused. Otherwise, hike 'em up. If you insist on being contrary, at least take your pants in at the crotch so it doesn't look as if you were smuggling contraband.

- Pants should fit in the back flat across the top of the buttocks, then follow its curve about halfway. When they follow all the way, we call them jeans, and they should cost a lot less.

◆ Look at your butt. Everyone else will.

10. *Most men dry-clean their suits too often.* The surest way to kill a good suit. The quickest way to age an inexpensive one. Do not dry-clean until a suit is visibly dirty or until you can't get the smell of cigarettes—or someone else you want to forget—out.

11. Most men iron their suits too often. Inexpensive ones often show their pedigree because overironing hastens the onset of that I-can-see-myself shininess. *Buy a portable steamer and steam your suits instead.* It's almost idiot-proof, certainly a lot easier to operate than an iron, while increasing a garment's longevity. And a steamer always belongs in your suitcase.

12. *The two parts of a suit do not come glued together.* You can and should wear them separately. Mix them, top and bottom, with other elements of your wardrobe. We used to call this stretching a buck. We now call this fashion.

FEET, DON'T FAIL ME NOW

BUYING SHOES

Considering what shoes have to do, men should know more about them than anything else they put on each day. After all, ill-fitting sweaters just make you look awful, but poorly fitted shoes chuck your concentration, ruin your day, and enable your chiropractor to build that gazebo next to the pool. Nevertheless, most men know more about Janet Reno than they do about shoes. That's too bad because—like men who study a menu as if it were a quiz, only to ask their wives "Honey, what should I have?"—some things you have to decide for yourself. No one can tell you how a shoe fits. You have to wear it.

◆ Men generally buy shoes only when they have to, one pair at a time, and then wear the hell out of them. Big mistake. Shoes are not made out of copper or chipboard. Socks are not usually made out of terry cloth. Feet sweat. A lot. Even more when they're in boots. Shoes need to dry out. And breathe. And be rotated. You have more than one tie? More than one suit? Assemble a wardrobe of shoes, if you want to wear any of them for a while.

- You don't need as many shoes as socks, but you need to have more shoes than Phillips screwdrivers.

- Shop in the afternoon, when your feet are wider. Don't wear athletic socks when trying on brogues. Wear the kind you will wear with the shoes.

- Knowing your shoe size is the same as knowing your suit size. It's just a starting point.

- New shoes are not sold with blister pads for a reason. They're supposed to fit now. Feel the need to break something in? Join the rodeo.

- Shoes will give a little in the width, not at all in the length, but fitting a shoe based solely on these criteria is like buying a suit because the jacket closes and you can zip up the pants. What you really should be checking is whether your foot feels good in the *last* of the shoe.

- The last is the name given to both the original wooden form used to shape the shoe (top to bottom, front to back), as well as to the final shape the leather takes once your foot replaces the wooden form inside the finished version. All shoes, even those mass-produced, are made on a last. Any discomfort within the finished last—instep, heel, bridge, vamp (how high the shoe rises on the instep)—can make you wish you were surfing, even if you never have before. Comfort in these areas is not negotiable. So it's not just about where the toe ends and whether the heel slips out of the loafer. In fact, because shoes have such varied front-end silhouettes, where the toe ends is not nearly so important as where the ball of the foot sits.

◆ Basically, you are choosing from three types of shoes:

—Italian shoes—designed to feel like slippers. They often have a glued bottom; are generally light, easy to pack, get creased quickly; and are hard to repair. Great for ballroom dancing, and fast conquests.

—English shoes—tend to have heavy leather on the upper part, which is stitched to a reinforced welted sole, making it a little stiff (though not painful) until the welting is pliant. Great for pacing, crossing one's legs, appearing formidable and responsible, and turning on one's heel for dramatic exits.

—Outdoor shoes—work boots, Timberlands, Doc Martens, and such are the footwear walking in rhythm at the moment. Versatile, affordable, durable (Doc Martens oil-resistant soles were developed for mechanics), and as butch as eating jalapeño peppers or being into candle wax, they go with everything. They look especially testosteronic when paired with soft suits, leather pants, and your new black Jeep Grand Cherokee, which you won't let the kids eat in the back of.

Retailers' consensus: Good dress shoes, whether English or Italian, cost $150 to $300 on the average; work boots, $85 to $165. Of course, you can go much higher on the former.

If you go much higher on the latter, you probably ought to match the color against your Range Rover.

♦ You are not Cinderella, but:

—If you have a high instep, low-vamped shoes like Chelsea (once called Beatle) boots may be cut too low across the top for you.

—Flat feet can make you feel tired after wearing no-support Italian loafers for just a few hours, and Western boots seem more treacherous than skating barefoot on dry ice. Generally, flat feet need a gently arched and roomier last.

—Work shoes can make narrow feet feel as if they were dragging along gravity boots.

—Just as they have dry and oily facial areas, most Americans have combination feet, i.e., D up front, B in back. American shoes tend to accommodate this problem. Most European shoes do not.

Because of these reasons, and the uniqueness of your own feet, try the shoes on—both of them (one foot is bigger than the other)—and keep them on. Walk in them. Sit in them. Walk again. Wait. Let your feet settle in. Then walk again. Take your time. Shoes do not lend themselves well to impulse buying, like fuzzy dice and K-Tel disco tapes "not sold in stores." Don't be intimidated by the salesman's low snit level. He's not going anywhere fast. Not with his hands smelling like that.

- Ideally, all shoes should be lined in leather, for absorption. Check inside. If they're not, pass. Now *that* should get him snitty.

- It's normal to go up a half size with boots. If they fit, you should be able to pull your heel right out. Wear boot socks, or at least thick cotton ones, because of the increased sweat. In fact, for the sake of all your shoes, never wear acrylic socks.

- You wash, iron, clean, and press the rest of your wardrobe. And none of it gets the beating shoes do. What makes you think you can get away with just polishing? Wooden shoe-trees were not invented to give Anthony Hopkins something to do in a Merchant Ivory film. They're the best way to protect your investment. They speed the drying process, deodorize, and prevent shoes from curling at the toe. They are as vital for maintaining the quality of shoes as flossing is for teeth.

- Plastic shoe-trees are the wire hangers of footwear.

- You have about eight hours to wipe off salt before it starts to burn leather. If you're approaching or past the zero hour, try cleaning the damaged area with diluted white vinegar.

- Saddle soap is for cleaning I-really-did-venture-some-where-that-justified-owning-an-all-terrain-vehicle ground-in dirt or untanned leather. It is very drying and not really for dress shoes. If you do use it, follow immediately with cream polish or Lexol, a leather conditioner.

- ·Liquid polish on good footwear is right up there with ketchup on foie gras. It drips, cracks, and does nothing for the leather. It's strictly for people who have dogs named Tige looking up from their heel.

- Paste polish is used primarily to enhance color. It does stain leather well. It also runs.

- Cream polish conditions leather, moistens, hides nicks. It's the right way to brush.

- Other people do see the bottoms of your shoes, or do you never cross your legs, big guy? (And I'll bet you kiss your horse.) Resole your shoes before you can see through the bottom.

- No matter what your dad told you, the right brown shoes look just fine with a black suit.

DENIM & EQUITY

BUYING JEANS

Jeans are perhaps America's greatest contribution to world culture, superseded only by jazz, big-budget movies, and homegrown artists like Ella Fitzgerald, Samuel Clemens, Bette Davis, Stevie Wonder, and Karen Carpenter. (You think her name is here for a joke, don't you? Well, when was the last time you attended a wedding—anywhere in the solar system—where they didn't play "We've Only Just Begun"? Thought so.)

Jeans were first made for California Gold Rush miners by a Jewish tailor (could you bust?) named Levi-Strauss, using a blue-dyed canvas imported de Nimes, France, which he'd been using to make tents and covered wagons. (If you failed to catch the origin of the word "denim" in the last sentence, maybe you should have bought a crossword puzzle book.)

Most people used to wear the same clothes every day. No longing sighs, please. (That's why Shakespeare's characters got away with so much mistaken identity merely by changing costumes.) Even without scent strips, it was a smelly world. And a tough one. Clothes had to last. Cute as they were, the rivets on jeans were designed to make seams indestructible and keep pockets from tearing, not to brand your bare skin when you folded pants straight from the dryer.

No matter how perennially hip Woody Guthrie has become, jeans were not fashionable for about a hundred years. Ladies on Nob Hill did not don them when they wanted to get down and ride the trolley. Jeans remained workers' duds throughout the Depression, available in one tubular width and fold-up-able length. If you weren't working, you weren't wearing them. Kids did not wear them to school unless they'd showed up right off the thresher. And despite the '50s mythology surrounding James Dean and *Grease*'s Rizzo, only JDs wore them to class, and they never went. Jeans hit the big time in the '60s as part of the counterculture. Turn on, tune in, drop out, zip up.

1.   Designers may be the worst thing that ever happened to jeans. Which is why the No. 1 rule of jeans shopping is: If there's a designer's name on the back, they're not really jeans. Oh, they're denim all right. And they have a jeans cut. But they're not jeans-jeans. Furthermore, why are you spending $455 on miner's pants? That's like paying $37 for pot roast. If you're guilty of this as well, get the jeans, eat the pot roast, buy the gold mine, who cares what you do?

2.   Regardless of how many variations and numerical categories come flapping down the boardwalk, finding the right jeans is a remarkably consistent process, because it all focuses on the crotch and the butt.

3.   In order to gauge this fit properly, no matter how you see them advertised or promoted, jeans are supposed to fit around the waist. As for the urge to buy them four sizes too big, if you can remember the world before John Grisham, yo, this trend should probably not concern you.

4.   Jeans are the original lift and separators. The right ones have the Merlinesque ability to make a fairly trim waist look trimmer, to make a round butt appear mouthwatering (yeah, we're talking about you, fella), and to veil an eager crotch in mystery. The wrong ones can make love handles stick out like chafing-dish holders, thighs resemble canned indigo hams, and wide rear ends capable of showing first-run films. Because there is no other single item in all of apparel cut in as many unstandardized ways, you must try jeans on before you buy them.

5.   What's more unappealing than a flat, droopy butt in an ill-fitting pair of jeans? (A red tie with a tuxedo? Kelsey Grammer in a thong?) You must look in the mirror from all directions once you try them on.

6.   If you are more than a size 38 (actually 36, but then the industry might collapse), you shouldn't wear jeans.

7.   Jeans should not break. Unlike trousers, the line should be clean from waist to ankle. This is not always an easy call when buying jeans needing to be shrunk to fit. Ask a salesperson how much they're going to. If the staff are too engrossed in their social life, figure an inch in the waist and two in the length, but it does vary from brand to brand. And the heat of your washer and dryer is also a factor. It really is a process of trial and error. Worse comes to worst, roll them up and tell folks you loved Sal Mineo. If you don't know who Sal Mineo was, you may be able to buy your jeans four sizes too big.

8. Rodeo riders wear their jeans (usually a pair of Wranglers) three to four inches too long, but that's because their pants ride up when they mount their broncos and they don't want to look unseemly before they're thrown. If imitating this choice makes you think it looks more authentic, get on that pony and ride. It will also make you look short.

9. If you're looking for a classic jeans silhouette, there are three kinds of legs: boot legs, tapered legs, straight legs.

10. Anorexics and flamingos look good in tapered legs. Everyone else looks about to tip over.

11. Boot legs are wider from the calf to the ankle so that you can pull your pants over your boots with no hassle. But unless you work with cattle, this is rarely a big worry.

12. Straight legs have the same width from knee to ankle. They have the cleanest line, though for those with muscular legs, the thigh's the limit. Recently developed straight-leg loose fits offer deliverance. Anyone else, from average height and build to tall and lean, will probably look best in straight legs.

13. Zippers and buttons are about preference. A lot of people think buttons are sexier—until they get stuck trying to undo one while not looking at it.

14. All major jeans companies cover all bases but they do maintain elements of a signature shape. Levi's tend to break in and soften fastest, fit great in the crotch. Lee jeans veer toward the most slimming in the hips. Wranglers are tough to tame, but fit neat in the butt, especially if you have a great one. If you don't, go back to Levi's.

15. Flannel jeans should be marketed as the adult's snowsuit.

16. Black jeans are the most versatile. Every suitcase—weekender or two-suiter—should pack a pair. A fresh pair can "pass" almost everywhere.

17. People used to be embarrassed by new jeans. Not anymore. Clean, unfaded, structured jeans are about as humiliating as a good job. Jeans with holes in them are about as impressive, and sexy, as an unemployment check.

18. White chocolate. Dress jeans. Both make equal sense.

19. Jeans look super with at least 470 other things. But not everything.

20. They don't belong on the same body as a tie.

21. There ought to be a summons for people who wear

them sockless with loafers. It's the Gold Card version of being faced with the crack of a bent-over handyman's butt.

22.   Jeans and patent leather work only with big burnt-blond hair and a tube skirt.

23.   Jeans shouldn't be paired with a dinner jacket. Sure, big stars do it. They also buy big houses near fault lines atop hills prone to mudslides.

24.   Dry-clean jeans? If you want people to think you live on Manhattan's Upper East Side and every meal you eat is brunch.

25.   After about a dozen washings, you can wash jeans with whites, in hot water and bleach, and age them faster, if that's your desire.

26.   Anyone who deliberately puts a crease in his jeans should be condemned to a life of tea sandwiches and escorting women who love only their halitosic dogs and slur their gimletted speech so badly even Dominick Dunne doesn't want to write about them anymore.

27.   Jeans are not the most comfortable pants you can buy. Beautifully cut wool crepe or silk crepe trousers are. But these days it would be easier to convince a kid transfixed by Nintendo that *Huckleberry Finn* is more fun.

BUYING UNDERWEAR

No matter what some women think, not every man walking down the street adjusting his crotch is thinking about nailing some babe. It's more likely his shorts don't fit.

They may be the first thing we put on and the last we take off, yet undershorts remain the forgotten garment. No matter that Marky Mark flaunting his Calvins spawned racks of ripped-abs imitators. Men still wear whatever is handy, or whatever they're handed. Consequently, undershorts are to a man's wardrobe what Susan Lucci is to daytime TV: ever present but disrespected. Used and ignored. However, unlike the Emmy Award–losing actress, underwear unexamined exacts revenge.

Sadly, repeatedly, men have discovered that something they pay little attention to becomes all they think about, and almost always too late. That's because men retain this image of Mom holding a plastic-wrapped three-pack between her two extended palms, clasped in a heartfelt entreaty to wear clean underwear. What Mom failed to add is that while cleanliness is next to godliness, underwear is next to something almost as important, so it's supposed to fit and feel good. You're a big boy now. Big and uncomfortable. Something has to change, besides your shorts. Like the way you acquire them.

1.   Try adjusting your attitude. *Underwear is clothing.* The communal brushoff—who sees it anyway?—not only is bogus but represents a Calvinist (no pun intended) denial of a basic pleasure. Nice underwear feels really good. Women know this. Men may, but they fall far short of indulging in such hedonism. They cringe at the thought of being overheard caring about their "unmentionables"—like a fatso facing cottage cheese—then obsess about their dress shirts. Where's the logic in going all out on a cashmere sport coat that never actually touches your skin, and then wearing it on top of a pair of discounted, slightly irregular $1.98 briefs that are going to bind you better than a carton of matzoh. Considering the geography, where should quality be job 1?

2.   Not surprisingly, women know something else men don't, which is why they have a variety of bras for the same pair of breasts. *Different undershorts suit different purposes.* You don't need the same support wearing a suit that you do playing squash. When you're loafing in a hammock on a Sunday, a baggy pair of boxers offers freedom. But watch the inexperienced try to stuff them into a pair of 501s. Men behave as if they were inscribed in The Book of Life as either a brief man or a boxer lover. Be fruitful and multiply your wardrobe.

3.   Man has rarely been responsible for his underwear drawer. Until recently, a woman bought 80 percent of these purchases. Now, it's closer to 60 percent (a trend undoubtedly influenced more by her decreased shopping time than his increased desire). While her sophistication and market dominance could be responsible for introducing you to higher-end lines (no pun intended), she's at an obvious disadvantage. How can anyone else tell if your underwear fits? When was the last time you bought her a bra? (The Frederick's of Hollywood kind doesn't count.) Even longtime bed partners don't always know how and where you want to tuck what you've got. It's very personal. *Buy your own shorts.* Unfortunately, because of health codes, you usually can't try skivs on or return them. So you have to start your purchasing cautiously. Still, there are ways to reduce short-circuiting.

4. *Don't lie about the size of your waist. Or the rest of you.* If you're that self-concious, rip the tags out when you get home and sew in other ones you've saved from days gone by, but this is no time for skimping. In fact, if you're buying underwear made in America, select a size larger, to allow for shrinkage. Even more precarious, however, is European sizing. An American small is size 28 to 32; a European small is more like 28 to 28.5. In addition, European men are built differently, generally smaller in the hips and in the rear. "Skintight" is a term that's comfortably applicable to leather pants and socks. (Doctors have even recommended looser shorts to remedy a low sperm count.) Before you grab that nifty bikini brief, make sure there's a place for everything. (No, that's not everything. What about your butt? Want to have panty lines? They'll look as good on you as they do on her.) This isn't going to the tailor. Conversely, just because boxers look roomier, don't assume they'll immediately make room for daddy. The inseam can come up so high as to divide and conquer, the fly can be set like a tower window, or there may be so much fabric in the seat that a frantic race to purge or urge winds up a mean game of hide-and-seek.

5.   *The right fabric can make your day.* Basic carded cotton is the industry standard. But it's not hard to find combed cotton, flannel, silk, cotton jersey, cashmere. The problem is, men haven't been trained to ask for something better. But if you're going to dress well, start at the bottom. You've fingered enough enviable suits, sweaters, and ties. Should a fabric feel pleasurable when you simply run your hand over it, imagine how it would feel brushing against you all day. There is underwear out there that feels so good you may have to excuse yourself from the meeting for a minute, if you can stand. Do not look at this as an extravagance. This is smart investing, not decadence. You might even make more money. Getting to the end of your day without wanting to pull your underwear over the top of your head can prompt an hour of overtime. It's very refreshing.

6.   *Do not buy fabrics that don't breathe.* Don't make you, or your loved ones, suffer.

7.   Underwear is not nearly as disposable as people think. If it were, no one would pay higher prices for the better stuff. The problem is, *you're probably overwashing yours.* The combination of America's obsessive quest for ultimate hygiene ("whiter than white") and its snickeringly adolescent attitude that in the end (no pun intended) anything connnected with sex is dirty has dictated that we pour bleach on our underwear as if we were being deloused. Too bad the stuff is usually made of thinner fabric than your other clothes. Too bad too, that, because it's cleaned more often than your other clothes, it's actually less dirty. Too bad three, that bleach destroys Lycra. Scalding water breaks down rubber, i.e., elastic. To keep your *gatkes* from falling down around your ankles, warm water will do nicely. Use bleach when it's been a rough day. It happens. Otherwise, go easy—these items long to be close to you.

8.   *There is nothing sexier on either sex than a great pair of underwear.* It shows an awareness of sensuality about yourself. It says you're not taking someone else for granted, that you care how they see you. Try answering the door in a pair. Try knocking on the door in a pair. When you absolutely, positively, have to have it, overnight. Sign right here. Don't worry about the pen.

BABY, IT'S COLD OUTSIDE

BUYING GLOVES, SCARVES, HATS

Go ahead and spring for the thickest shearling or the downiest anorak, but forget about protecting everything else your new coat doesn't and you're going to freeze your everything else off. "Cold hands, warm heart" is a real cute aphorism. Try getting past it when you're out of fire logs. As long as frostbite is an option, it's best to realize that accessories are necessities you don't have to hang up.

GLOVES

◆ Unlined leather gloves are the most devilishly sexy (the best ones, called murderer's gloves, are those without the roomier side panels for the fingers), but they're not very warm. Cashmere and wool-lined gloves are, and since the price isn't much higher for what's softer and lighter, go cashmere.

◆ Double-lined gloves—leather on the outside, a wool liner on the inside—are bulkier but warmer still, because they're really two gloves in one.

Unlined gloves are devilishly sexy, but not warm.

- The worst lining for a glove, though, is rabbit fur. It's like trapping your hands inside that cheap chubby your high school girlfriend wore, only the good stuff's not in there anymore. Now the only skin you're copping a feel off of is matted and oily, like a drunk's toupee. And your hands are going to cold-sweat like a stand-up blowing his one shot with Dave.

- Wool gloves offer variety, weightlessness, and—essential for those who keep losing the left ones—economy. Scientists, however, claim the most efficient hand covers are mittens. They would. Try reading a paper, finding a token, dialing a pay phone, or navigating anything with an air bag, and you'd sooner wear handcuffs straight out of the refrigerator.

- Purchasing suede gloves is a splendid idea for those men who can't find enough things for their valet to do.

- Be as exacting about fit as if you were buying that new catcher's mitt for the kid's Little League father-and-son playoffs. That extra space at the end of the fingers isn't supposed to be there unless you're expecting sudden surges of growth.

◆ How should gloves fit? Take a guess.

SCARVES

◆ It's not a collar that didn't get sewn on. A scarf is supposed to keep your neck warm, so don't drape it over you like a prayer shawl.

◆ If it doesn't wrap around your neck at least twice, don't bother.

◆ Go gently into that good-for-nothing night. The neck's derma is thin, easily irritated skin. Cashmere, silk, cotton, and viscose blends are kind to it. Polyester, shetland, or lambswool costs less but can turn the area around your Adam's apple into a topographical map of Balaclava after the Charge of the Light Brigade. This is not how you exhibit bravado, or have you forgotten that John Wayne wore cotton kerchiefs?

◆ It's a lot harder to pull off two coats than two scarves.

◆ Can't duplicate those intricate knots in the ads? Take a long scarf. Double it. Place it, folded, round your neck. Pull both loose ends through the curve on the opposite end. Fling ends over opposite shoulders. If you've done good, you'll look like a Lillehammer Olympian. If you've done wrong, you'll look as if you and Bea Arthur were separated at birth.

HATS

- Though percentages vary widely, you lose so much body heat through your head that any covering is fine. Should you look great in hats, it's time to shine. If you're like most who don't, put it this way: You're not going to look so great with blue lips and a red nose either. Cut your losses.

- Everyone makes fun of earlaps. Till they wear them. Let them call you Elmer Fudd. How often did he catch the flu?

- Fedoras blow away. Baseball caps are thin and often perforated. Hoods make bag ladies and store detectives nervous. A watch cap is as good as it gets. Don't wear it like a yarmulke. Pull it over the ears and down the forehead. Cashmere watch caps are almost too cool for this lifetime.

- Fur hats work. Ask Solzhenitsyn.

LOVING CARE AND FROSTED TIPS

◆ Do not pull the wool liner out of a double-lined glove to wash in Woolite or you're asking for Rubik's Five Finger Exercise. Give the whole thing over to be dry-cleaned.

◆ Never pull a loose thread from a scarf or sweater. Wrap the yarn around a flathead pin to pull it through to the inside.

◆ "Hand knit" means about as much as "home cooking." It's a type of production, not a standard of achievement, and can apply to a roll of weaving that's been cut up, pieced, and sewn together into sweaters. Fit and quality of yarn are more important.

◆ Gore-Tex, Thinsulate, Polartex mean more than "hand knit" when you're shivering. And you thought space exploration was a waste of federal funds.

◆ Coatracks and hooks look easy and homey, but they're terrible for coats and sweaters unless you want to play "What Hump?" Use wood hangers for coats. Fold a sweater and store it flat.

A Note on Long Underwear: The winter essential almost nobody sees is a godsend in silk because it weighs virtually nothing, is completely nonrestrictive, is not nearly as expensive as you think, and feels so good you may forgo all the rest of this stuff and never budge till spring creeps over the windowsill.

A MEDIUM IS THE MESSAGE—

BUT SO IS AN EXTRA LARGE

WHAT YOUR WARDROBE SAYS ABOUT YOU

Go ahead. Try.

Get rid of all the obvious indicators.

Turn your funny-sloganed T-shirts inside out.

Take a seam ripper to every proper-name-emblazoned back pocket in your closet.

Make your own label-less clothes.

It won't make any difference.

We know what you're thinking. What you choose to wear and how you choose to wear it reveal more personal data than a TRW. Thought you were exposing yourself in the shower only? Watch what you wear. Stand by your clothes. Your slips will be showing.

THE COVER	THE REVELATION
◆ **New York Mets cap**	◆ I'm a native who doesn't want to know from the Bronx or Brooklyn. In fact, I'd kill to live in West Palm.
◆ **Yankee cap**	◆ Who cares about base-ball? Navy blue goes with everything.
◆ **Baseball cap, turned around, on:**	
—Type A, i.e., model, MTV VJ, JFK, Jr.	—I'm not hung up on my celebrity and beauty because I know you are.
—Type B, i.e., guys over 40	—Betcha I'm dope. Betcha can't see the bald spot. Canya?
◆ **Beret**	◆ I wish I were in Paris. I wish I'd been in Vietnam. I wish I were anywhere I didn't have to wear this beret.

◆ **Earlapped headgear worn with laps down**	◆ My self-confidence is on a par with this hat.
◆ **Long ponytail**	◆ I want to make lots of money, but please don't tell anyone.
◆ **Short ponytail**	◆ I love making money. I can buy art.
◆ **"Regular man's haircut— not too much off the top"**	◆ My wife buys all my underwear. Shesmagirl!
◆ **Parted down the middle**	◆ I'd subscribe to *Granta* if someone would tell me what it is.
◆ **Sides buzzed, top dreaded**	◆ Don't worry, be happy. And watch my show on Fox.
◆ **Totally shaved**	◆ My options were this or looking like Lonnie's ex.
◆ **Mustache**	◆ Everything was better in the old days.
◆ **Goatee**	◆ Why *were* we in Vietnam anyway?

◆ **Diamond stud earring**	◆ I got a new Camaro.
◆ **Colored-stone earring**	◆ I got an old Camaro.
◆ **Thin gold-hoop earring**	◆ It's not too much, is it? And I take it out when I'm at work.
◆ **Thick gold-hoop earring**	◆ They can't fire me.
◆ **Two silver-hoop earrings, one in each ear**	◆ Freelance.
◆ **Small brushed-gold wire-rim glasses**	◆ Love A&E.
◆ **Aviators**	◆ Aerosmith in concert, man. Never miss an issue of *Rolling Stone*.
◆ **Half-glasses**	◆ If these menus weren't printed so damn tiny . . .
◆ **Sexual innuendos on a T-shirt**	◆ I bought the Rush Limbaugh book. Nah, I just bought it.
◆ **Yellow oxford cloth shirt**	◆ No one'll ever guess I bought a half dozen at a closeout sale.

- **Loosened tie**

- **Three-button suit worn with knit shirt**

- **$1,700 suit and button-down white oxford**

- **Dark solid suit, thin lapel, tab collar**

- **Dark double-breasted pinstripe, starched white shirt, red tie**

- **One-button wool crepe, white shirt with spread collar, silk tie**

- **All-weather sack suit worn with "Dale Carnegie" tie (any cravat sporting embroidered animals)**

- Forget the details. Give me the big picture. And don't ever call me cheap.

- Women like me because I look sophisticated. I *think* I can act sophisticated.

- Why didn't I buy in early on Disney?

- You could eat off the top of my desk, but if you do, don't make a mess.

- "If your bank says no, Champion says yes."

- Peter Jennings is God.

- I can conversate with anyone. Even if they don't want to.

- **Chalk-striped suit, slicked hair, thin-soled imported loafers**

- I have arrived! Where's everyone else?

- **Unribbed short-sleeved knit shirt, triple-pleated shorts, fake Top-Siders**

- Stop fighting back there! Because I'm the dad, that's why.

- **Tweed jacket, plaid shirt, knit tie**

- The Woodman used to be so funny. Ever see *Bananas?*

- **Brass-button blazer, chinos, $125 running shoes**

- I'm an active kinda guy. You gonna eat that?

- **Three-button putty-colored wool-twist suit with brushed wool shirt**

- Talk business for a minute and I can still write this off.

- **Four-button cocoa and stone-herringbone suit, anthracite cashmere crewneck, multi-eyelet boot shoes**

- I work on Seventh Avenue, but it's not the real me.

- **A Savile Row nipped-waist worsted, blue shirt, white collar, French cuffs, tie bar, foulard**

- I *am* relaxed.

- **White T-shirt, blue jeans, $125 basketball sneakers**

- **Matching nylon running suit, fanny pack**

- **Plaid duffle coat, sweatshirt, catalogue-bought khakis**

- **Straw cowboy hat, hooded sweatshirt, slipping jeans with too much stitching on pockets, gold chain**

- **Black studded motorcycle jacket, black leather vest, silk T-shirt, white jeans**

- **Black leather jacket, no shirt, ripped jeans, chaps, concho belt, lizard cowboy boots**

- **Big black work boots**

- I gotta be my own man. Are you gonna finish that?

- Is this the smoking section?

- I always watch *Saturday Night Live*, alone, always.

- Got any Tums?

- Drives a brand-new fire-engine-red Nissan Sentra, with dual cam.

- You should see me on my bike. In fact, you should only see me on my bike.

- I'm glad everyone's wearing them again. They're so me.

- **Black T-shirt, black jeans, black cowboy hat, black Western boots**

- **Black all the time**

- Hi, I'm Clint Black.

- Everyone says I'm talented.

TAKE TIME

DYING OF THIRST

SKIN CARE

You didn't think it mattered, did you? You wash, you dry, and you're out of there. Your skin? What about it? It's clean. Used a new blade. Even put on some of that aftershave balm you got for Christmas. What else is there to do? Oh, not that gunk she wears. Shmearing eye creams. Calculating the right number sunblock. You got a hat. Besides, you don't burn—you tan.

Except the mirror's stopped sending you off with a "Looking good, kiddo." The media harangues about ozone layers, UV rays, Retin-A, and the dramatic rise in melanoma are getting to you. Your skin's a little flaky. Sometimes, it's itchy. You burn.

Face it. You're getting older.

She's getting better.

You? You're not so sure.

It's time you knew.

A man can't afford to treat his skin any differently than the way a woman treats hers. Don't want to hear it, do you, macho man? You're thinking, Skip this chapter and who'll be the wiser? Well, some folk might, considering you're no longer in as much devil-may-care company as you think. A decade ago, cosmetics firms couldn't get male focus groups to discuss skin treatment—they dismissed everything as greasy. But now the boomers have turned 40, and they don't like feeling it, or looking it. Suddenly there is receptivity. According to a 1991 Simmons Market Research report, 49.1 percent of men admitted using hand and body lotion. Add on a few more points for those not telling the truth, and a few more for the widespread dissemination of information in the intervening years, and there's not that big a rally round your flag, boy. Keep scratching if you want to. Tell others it's due to bewilderment. But you can still stave off prune season if you act now.

◆ Stop washing with those banded quartets of detergent soaps sold in discount drugstores for next to nothing. This is all the skin factory you're ever going to have, and like it or not, it's in the first stages of a work slowdown, so be extra nice to it. Gentler glycerin soaps or impurity-cleansing clay soaps are better, and not just for the face. Recommended products: Origins Skin Diver (you'll like it, it's black), Kiehl's Liquid Castile Soap, Clinique Bar Soap.

◆ Long hot showers and baths actually dehydrate. Keep both of them warm and short, unless you're trying to soak away the urge to commit a violent act on a coworker or paramour.

◆ When you wash, if you're not scruffing or exfoliating, and haven't retarred the driveway, pretend it's someone else's skin. Go easy. Squeaky clean is for dishes.

◆ You can't go without moisturizing anymore. Your skin isn't producing the humectants it used to. You don't need gunk. But you do need help. Most men's hydrating products are either oil-free or have low oil content; are light, absorbed almost instantly; and have savvy, nonthreatening packaging—usually in austere steel blue, charcoal gray, or burled brown—for those squeamish about medicine cabinet espionage. Naturally, if you are used to using nothing, anything may seem a little too on-your-face at first, but you have to stop thinking that that tight, just-rinsed-off-deodorant-soap feeling is the ideal.

◆ Your top layer of dead skin now tends to clump and cling rather than flake off. Shaving exfoliates that part of your face, but as for the rest of you, you're covered in it. There are two ways to get rid of it:

—For the face, there are chemical exfoliators employing either alpha hydroxy (a fruit-based acid) or salicyllic acid (derived from tree bark). They slough off the useless layer, invigorate the new skin, and allow it to breathe.

—For the body, mechanical scrubs like loofah bars, containing granulation, strip scaliness off the rest of you, and should be used twice a week, or gently on the second day of a sunburn (or you wind up moisturizing dead skin). Once again, conserve your strength. Let the soap do the work.

◆ The goal of moisturizing is not just to put moisture in, but to keep moisture from getting out. Put lotion on as soon as you get out of the shower, when your skin is still damp.

- You cannot use the same moisturizer on your body as on your face. Your body needs more outside assistance. For example, your legs have no sebaceous oil glands. Sweat from shoes and socks only makes things worse. Having trouble getting used to the feeling of a moisturizer? That's because you have to allow it a few minutes to sink in. Shave. Comb your hair. Floss. Dance around the room naked. Relax. It will go away.

- If your skin is oily, washing too much with harsh, drying products won't necessarily help, because the body's clever little oil glands react to negative feedback and kick into overtime. What you should be looking for are products that balance your PH levels, not Sahara-ize you.

- Loofah your elbows daily and attack the undersides of your feet with a pumice stone once a week if you're tired of their having the texture of beach glass. Regular body lotion isn't strong enough for the ugly parts. Look for oilier products—often containing shea butter and avocado oil—made specifically for callused areas.

- Don't need eye cream, huh? Guess who needs it more than women do? Eyes are surrounded by the tenderest skin on the face. Women at least use makeup, usually with SPF factors. Men, however, have always ignored the area, and that's where the lines come first. Still refuse to use? Okay, there are options. Get rid of those hip little sunglasses. Get wraparounds. Find those aviators. And then: no sun, no stress, no wincing, no smiling. Or: there's always surgery.

- Look at the faces of those actors who've had work done and look incredible. Then look at their hands. Hands are age's way of saying gotcha. Better moisturize them too.

- You can't face the summer sun without protection either. Exposure is constant, and wearing a hat is of limited effectiveness, since the sun reflects up from the water, the sand, even the sidewalk.

- Many tanning products say "waterproof" or "water resistant." And they are, provided you're Norwegian and vacationing along the North Sea in October. But as long as you're sweating, on a beach or a tennis court, you should reapply *every hour*. Don't, and your tan may soon resemble one of Jackson Pollock's later works.

- Using straight baby oil? Or, better yet, with iodine? Ever see bacon left too long in the pan? You're on your way. As for the myth that real men don't use sunscreen—real men get skin cancer. Your move.

- You have about one hour to save yourself after being out too long in the harsh sun. Avoid the blue-glass jars of stuff that feels cool and the spray stuff that stings. Take a lukewarm bath with a soluble bath and body oil. Then moisturize constantly. Rub a dozen aloe leaves on your skin. Drink enough water to float a tug. Pray.

- If you get a sunburn, don't shave, don't scrub. Try a moisturizing mask. Stay indoors. Avoid cologne. Buy a caftan.

- Though many people know enough to stay off the beach at high noon, remember that UV rays are ever-present, whether it's 9 A.M. or 4 P.M. Sunblocks, even numbers as high as 35, don't mean you can stay in the sun all day. When they are tested, they are applied to the subjects like paste, so a little dab won't do ya. And their efficacy at staving off melanoma is now being questioned. By the way, anything over 15 is like trying to make water wetter. However, you can get a tan even while wearing 25. Want to be fully blocked? Get dressed.

- For clean, healthy, younger-looking skin, as much water as you can drink is not enough.

- A skin-care regimen will add 15 minutes to your entire day, tops, which finally gives you somewhere to put all that time you claim to be saving on baked potatoes with your new microwave. That's a quarter of an hour for looking a few years younger. You've made worse deals.

REMEMBER THE MANE

IT'S ONLY HAIR. YEAH, RIGHT.

Is there a greater right-between-the-eyes reminder that your youth is checking out—leaving no forwarding address—than the first time you see a drain clogged with your own hair? That's it. It's over. The nightmare begins. No more looks back. No more dates. Nothing to run your fingers through for effect, as if anyone will hang around long enough to have a conversation with you. God hates you.

Why the big deal over a mass of dead follicles? Because, for 50 years, hair has been tossed around as our most visible symbol of virility. Of all the myths and legends postwar American men fell victim to, none has been more potent than the Samsonian ideal of manhood.

The evidence was clear. Elvis had lots of hair. So did Don Drysdale, Rock Hudson, Charles Van Doren, Norman Mailer, Michael Landon, Robert Redford. Why were we so sure Warren Beatty and John Kennedy had bedded all those women? How could they not, with all that hair? Meanwhile, on the cue ball side, there stood only Yul Brynner, an exotic, barefoot aberration whose appeal was undoubtedly helped by the fact that he seemed to be the only man in Siam with a waist.

Look how flattened all those pompadours got when Marilyn Monroe married Arthur Miller. Why didn't it track that a world-famous actress might want to marry the man who had written what many regarded as the Great American Play of his generation? Because he had no hair. Balding was the guy Marilyn was supposed to dump for Robert Mitchum. The guy every woman would dump. Balding meant the sputtering authority of Colonel Klink, the haplessness of Mel Cooley, the sexual appetite of Bub on *My Three Sons* . . . The defoliated never got their own TV show. The defoliated were always second banana.

No wonder the potential of Rogaine, first released as Minoxidil a decade ago, was so brazenly exploited by the press that few listened to the lower expectations set by its manufacturer, the Upjohn Company. The information—that one had to suffer through dry scalp, months of vellous, baby-fine hair, an expensive prescription not covered by medical insurance, waiting a year to experience any kind of moderate growth, with less than a 1 in 2 chance of that happening, but a guarantee that as soon as you stop drip-dropping the stuff on your head, you're back to square one—seemed as ignored as Jane Hathaway was by Jethro.

But between the time the sitcoms of the '60s left the Top 10 and their revival, like Lazarus with a laugh track, two decades later on Nick at Nite, two major cultural shifts have occurred: The generation that saw these shows when first run have undergone a benign form of shock treatment while advancing toward middle age.

Lo and behold. With a combed-forward-but-fooling-no-one-haircut, Kevin Costner becomes one of the most popular stars in the world. With a dyed-scalp-to-match-whatever's-left, Bruce Willis pockets $15 mil a movie with greater ease than you get reimbursed for petty cash. Jack Nicholson gets to stalk Michelle Pfeiffer. Ed Harris, John Malkovich, Danny Glover, William Hurt, and Ted Danson all have name-above-the-title status. And regardless of how many anointed charlatans intone, "Bond. My name is James Bond," Sean Connery's true voice remains the only one we'll ever willingly believe, even when his mustache is the only hair left on his head.

The generation rediscovering these shows has created different signposts of vitality. As one of youth's few heroes, Michael Jordan embodies commitment, success, passion, sportsmanship, Gatorade; but most of all, he radiates health and power. America's most admired athlete also happens to be a chrome-dome.

Sparked by our insatiable fascination with the Olympics, Americans now see shaving down—which swimmers, runners, divers, wrestlers, and gymnasts routinely do for comfort and speed—as a sign of vitality. Woman no longer dismiss a man with thinning hair if he's in shape. In fact, strong features with a sparse field of dreams are regarded by many as very sexy.

The effect of this reappraisal is most apparent—where else?—on MTV. Hours go by when it appears as if half the guys appearing on its videos, promos, and dance programs have shaved heads. With guys blessed with full heads of hair choosing to shave theirs, the man who's losing or has lost his should exchange time spent whining for a knee-walking pilgrimage to Guadaloupe.

For those who haven't enough trade-inable frequent flyer

miles and still wouldn't mind a celestial stay for what strands they've still got:

- The best thing you can do to maintain and accentuate what's left is to get a good, sympathetic haircut. Go to a skilled cutter. Keep it short, cut it blunt. Your hair will look fuller and less patchy, and be easier to take care of.

- Thinking of growing it long, are you? Skillfully hide the bare patches, right? You fool. The last time you had it that way, I'll bet some girl said you looked like Boz Scaggs. Life was sweet then, wasn't it, like something out of Dickens, one of the guys who takes money from widows and orphans. Leave the thinning pates and ponytails to characters in Kurosawa films.

- Thinning hair tends to be dry. Do not wash yours with detergent shampoo.

- In every step of your hair grooming, keep to a minimum the products that contain alcohol.

- Use moisturizing shampoos that contain ingredients like shea butter or lauryl sulfate and/or ones with a botanical base. Screw up your courage, be a brave warrior, and *ask* the woman behind the counter what she recommends. Don't forget to hang around long enough for the answer.

- Do not blow-dry hair when it's soaking wet. That's when it's most fragile. If you have the time, let it dry naturally about three quarters of the way. Then blow-dry, first with your fingers, then with a brush. If you don't have the time, start with a fresh towel, not the one you just used to dry off the rest of you, and towel dry for about a minute and a half.

◆ Don't blow-dry dry hair. Don't blow-dry hair you've just plastered with oil or petroleum-based products either. You're scorching the former, frying the latter. Add all that stuff after you've fluffed. If you need to massage something in first, try a little conditioning cream.

◆ Don't try to give your hair volume. You'll look like your mother, or worse, when you're back-lit, like *The Song of Bernadette.*

◆ Don't grease your hair down for illusions of density either. The Gekko look is as flat as the dollar. Trust what you have left to do all it can do. Be nice to it, or it will leave you crying.

◆ Take care of your scalp. You have probably never given it a minute's thought, but you'd notice a difference if you did something to clean and stimulate it. Massaging is a start. Scalp treatments, some of which take a grand total of 60 seconds, are even better.

◆ Hats, while effective against the sun for your hair, work against your scalp, resulting in severe dryness. What you think may be dandruff could just be dry scalp.

- Bare heads can be shiny. Bare spots should not be.

- Can't stand being called "the silver fox"? Don't trust sprays, comb-ins, brush-ons, shampoo-outs. Dye it. Except don't try doing it yourself, no matter how nice and easy the instructions read in the harsh light of Walgreen's. And don't suggest a girlfriend or spouse do it. Women can get away with hair that looks oddly unnatural. You couldn't even take the razzing the last time you unwittingly wound up with clear polish on your manicure.

  Don't be chintzy. Have a professional work on your head, a colorist who is familiar with dyeing men's hair. Besides, no matter what you've laughed at in old movies, beauty shop folk are tighter-lipped than friends and lovers.

- Beware. No one has truly black hair.

- If you want to try a hair weave, or a toupee, both of which are better than many people think, you have to be willing to make a commitment to it, and take care of it better than if it were a 1965 Mustang. Why better? Because no one will laugh at you if you don't wash the Mustang. Rugs and weaves require constant maintenance (in the case of the former, it's best to have more than one), hair matching, re-knotting, tightening, and cutting your own hair appropriately. You can never treat it hastily, as you do other areas of grooming when you're in a rush. If you haven't brushed your teeth, there's always gum, or the silent treatment. Treat your faux top the same way and the options are pity or a paper bag.

- Stay away from sex partners who behave like animals. You may get off on the screaming part, but let's see how hot you trot when they start to pull.

IT'S GROWING

HAIR CARE, EVERYWHERE ELSE

You sit there expounding on new directions, new dreams, new goals. She's not listening. Not even looking at you. Actually, she *is* looking at you, but not in the eye.

"You have a hair growing out of the middle of your cheek," she says with disgust. "A long golden, brownish hair, like the kind on your head, but it's on your face. Get rid of it."

"Where? Show me," you declare, tugging randomly. "I can't see it. Pull it."

"No way!" says she.

"I thought you loved me. Pull it," you demand in official, city-hall's-behind-me tones.

She reaches over, yanks, flails, and flicks it away with an "Ucch," as if she'd jerked her hand out of a Roach Motel. "Don't let it happen again!" she grouses in tones that now bespeak a future more tweezed than dreamt.

You're over 40? It'll be back.

No matter how commercials rhapsodize, analyze, and prophesy about the prospect of bouncy follicles shimmering with life, the only field of dreams they're in praise of is the batch that springs forth around the top of your head (which, by the way, is as dead as rope). Unfortunately, hair is capable of sprouting just about anywhere else, and the older you get, the more inventive and invasive growth patterns become. Well, you can wax your shoulders, you can wear socks, but what about all that other stuff emanating everywhere around your kisser.

FATHER KNEW ZIP

HOW TO SHAVE

Pop taught you everything you know about shaving, didn't he? That's your problem right there.

How are you fixed for blades? Remember Gunilla Knut- son? Dad does. She was this Amazonian Scandinavian blonde who'd appear on TV along with this guy lathered in Noxzema. "Take it doff, take it dall off," she'd purr Nordicly as he flipped a razor across his cheek as if it were scooping up warm ice cream, to the beat of a pop instrumental called "The Stripper." One splash of water and two slaps of aftershave later, Gunilla was stroking the dimpled fellow's smooth-as-iced-vodka chin, lying languid as a herring in his lap.

So who's cooing over your shoulder as you click in a new blade? When was the last time someone wanted to hang around and watch you initiate something as bloody, torturous, scarring, time-consuming, and ultimately fruitless as shaving. That's because there is no other regimen in a man's life so perpetuated by myth and bad advice. Your dad may be a great guy, but he probably knows as much about his face as he does about Scandinavian blondes.

1. *The key to a great shave is proper skin care.* If time were on your side, you'd be shaving in the evening, when your face is oilier, softer; when you're not rushed; and when your skin could heal while you sleep. But it's too late. Most men react to radical changes in grooming habits the way high school students treat a substitute teacher. So we'll play it your way.

2. It's still necessary to start the preparation in the evening. While you're asleep, your face rubs on sheets probably laundered in detergent. Steam heat parches your skin of whatever moisture hasn't already been absorbed by the pillowcase. Meanwhile, the better the condition of your skin, the better your shave. *Sleep with a humidifier on in the bedroom,* especially in the winter. And another thing. *Apply a moisturizer before bed.* Oh, come on. You don't have to look all white and greasy the way Gladys Kravitz did each night spying on Darrin and Samantha in *Bewitched.* A good moisturizer gets absorbed into the skin in three minutes. No one will know. And you may be surprised how cool it is to wake up with your face not feeling as if you'd wrapped it in the sports section.

3. In case you've never given it much thought, *shaving is taking a knife to your skin and ripping some of it off.* Plain enough? Such action actually causes the top layer to exfoliate, which is good—and it's a major reason why men's skin, though twice as tough as women's, ages less quickly. However, before giving this surface peel a chance to heal, you have to do it all over again. Scrape an elbow, or skin a hand, and you'd baby it. Then treat your face the same way. Anything harsh or full of chemicals—waxes, alcohols, perfumes—has no business being anywhere near that mug.

4. Drugstore shelves are full of stuff to shave with. Considering what's in most of them, you're better off shaving with hair conditioner. A razor should glide across your beard. In fact, it should go so smoothly that you could actually shave without a mirror. But rather than encouraging us to invest in quality products, elders and ad agencies have brainwashed us with a host of faux axioms. Use hotter water. Shave in different directions. Change the blade. Stretch your skin with the other hand. Buy whatever's on sale. No wonder you end up covered with pieces of toilet paper. Forget what you know:

- *Never shave with scalding water.* It breaks capillaries. It dries skin. Cuts happen more frequently. Either steam your face, place a warm washcloth on it, use a moisturizing scrub to soften the skin and make the beard stand up, or rub some scalp oil in. Save the boiling water for the Melitta.

- *Use a superior shave cream.* One face is the allotment from Portion Control. Make it last. Spend a few bucks. Roy's World Class Shaving Cream, Kiehl's Ultimate Brushless Shave Cream, Clinique Cream Shave, Aramis Lab Series Maximum Comfort Shave Cream, and Men by Geoff Thompson's Licorice Shave (anise is a natural antiseptic for the face) are five examples of products that feel radically different even before you shave. And once you do, it's hands-down-so-that's-it-where-have-you-been-all-my-tired-life no contest. Employ a product that contains glycerin, chamomile, aloe vera, almond oil, allantoin, and/or olive oil, and the blade glides, just the way Gunilla likes it. The shave is closer. The shave is faster. The result doesn't resemble the opening of *ER*. And since you use less of the better shave creams, the cost per shave adds up to much less of an extravagance than you originally thought.

◆ *As soon as that blade tugs, throw it out.* Like it or not, your razor will tell you how many shaves you get per blade. Every beard is different. How blades are stored varies. Stop trying to get your money's worth. You're paying for it with your profile. And dispose of the disposables immediately. They're like using a pen knife to carve a turkey.

◆ *Don't pull on your skin.* No yanking, no tugging, no making faces as if you were re-creating the climax from a Bruce Lee film. All this does is promote age lines, breaks elasticity, and helps skin sag. Be gentle. Pretend someone else is shaving you, like, maybe, Sweeney Todd. Just kidding.

◆ *Don't shave against the grain.* You shouldn't have to if you're using a quality shave cream and blade. Otherwise, it's like taking a scissors blade to the back side of a ribbon. The way a ribbon curls, that's how you get ingrown hairs.

- ◆ *Don't shave in front of a magnifying mirror.* Face fact: You have a beard. Try to shave too close and you're going to irritate your skin real bad. A regular mirror is fine. What you see is what they get.

- ◆ *Take your time.* Screw this up and it doesn't matter what suit you put on.

5.   Okay, you've attacked and now you're one big surface wound. So, what did Dad tell you to apply? Aftershave—alcohol of the lowest kind, combined with skin-irritating, synthetically made fragrance—which you're going to *slap* on until it stings like hell. What a man! What a guy! What a jerk.

Would you buy a shampoo that burned or soap that stung? Then why are you torturing yourself with something guaranteed to make you dance without a beat? *Never put alcohol on your face. Never put fragrance on it. You just hurt it. Now soothe it.*

Once again, you'll benefit from a product employing several of the following: aloe vera gel, camphor, calendula, gentian, allantoin, lemon extract, clove, even marshmallow. Products like Kiehl's herbal toners, Roy's aftershave, Men's Lemon Moisture Gel, and Aramis Lab Series shave balm will stave off the redness (which actually is due more to the aftershave than the shave) and minimize bumps. Should you cut yourself, *stay away from irritating styptic pencils.* A spot of any kind of tightening clay masque (Kiehl's, Queen Helene) works miracles in minutes. Or just use a bit of tissue and be patient.

6. *Use a moisturizer during the day.* The biggest and most dangerous myth is that men don't need skin protection. But ozone layer depletion and pollution are not gender-specific. Everyone these days needs protection. And no one needs to look any more weathered by time than he already is. By the way, stroke moisturizer on upward. Gravity is already taking care of the other direction.

For those who think man wasn't meant to shave. A beard is not so simple a solution, due to the disturbing realization that most men's beards and mustaches are textured more like their pubic hair than what's on their head. And the coarser, curlier, and tighter the beard, the more problems you have. No matter what you're daydreaming, a beard can't grow like an untended garden. The skin doesn't get to breathe, you perspire, food gets caught in it, the wind is drying. Before you know it, you're pretty itchy. And if you're itchy, think how it feels to someone else.

Trimming a beard is an exacting education of trial and painful error—your haircutter should show you how—but maintenance is easier. *Shampoo your beard with a mild non-detergent shampoo. Never use soap. Always condition it.* There are products on the market specifically for softening beards (Roy's and Kiehl's are two superior brands), and you should use massage oil for the scaliness that develops on the skin underneath. Don't overshampoo. Twice a week for a beard is enough. But condition it each time you wet it. And groom (brush, comb, massage) your beard more often than you do your hair. If you can't run your fingers through it, do you think Gunilla would want to?

HOW CAN YOU SEE, IT'S SO DARK IN THERE?

NOSE HAIR

Your best friends won't tell you. And they should. Because even braidable nose hairs aren't always easy to spot. By you anyway. The best way to check for the start of a second-tier mustache is to pinch your nostrils and pull up, and see what's wafting in a magnifying mirror. Getting rid of them is not nearly as carefree.

The coward's way out is offered by battery-operated nose hair clippers, which look like a hard plastic bottle of nasal spray. They're absolutely painless, and will eliminate finger-pointing, but they really give only a buzz cut.

Small barber scissors are superior, but you need a flair, which is going to require practice, and poking.

Falling somewhere between the two is a battery-operated clipper that looks like a black Magic Marker with small shark's teeth on the end. It's pretty good once you get used to the foreplay-with-no-follow-through tingle.

The most effective as well as the most painful way to re-move nose hair, however, is to get into the shower, put a squootch of fragrance-free moisturizer up your nose, wait a bit, take a pair of tweezers, and keep pulling hairs until there are none left to be seen in the glass. Do it when you're alone. Loved ones shouldn't know you're capable of such language.

Note: Despite it napalmic effect, some dermatologists caution against tweezing on the grounds that the irritation level is high enough to possibly cause infection on sensitive skin. If you have a skin doctor, check with him. But if your nostrils start looking like somebody's storing hula skirts in there, don't come crying here.

REPEAT THAT, PLEASE?

EAR HAIR

One of the most distinctive signs of growing venerable is the random harvest suddenly thriving on top of and inside your ears. For the former, you do need a magnifying mirror, a razor, and some shave cream. (Never shave any body hair dry. You'll end up with what looks like site-specific carpet burns.) However, don't ever cut hair you can't see. Ask your barber— excuse me, stylist—to trim what's in your ears. Don't move.

THE UNFURRIED

BROWS

Some guys like a single-lane stretch of highway over their orbs. Live and be well. Others should wax the small space between the eyes, a less arduous and risky process than tweezing, and lasting longer than shaving. Do not use a product like Nair on your face. There are specially designed depilatories for more fragile derma. They are usually pink and aren't found near the Mennen. Deal with it. Or ask your hair cutter to.

Another sign of dotage is the surprise eyebrow hair corkscrewing like wisteria up your forehead. Tweeze it or razor-cut it. If brows are merely unruly and you're averse to minor surgery, a little lip balm, eye balm, or petroleum jelly will arch them back in place.

The latter two are also great on lashes after skiing or anytime excessive wind makes them dry and itchy. Several prominent pharmacists swear eye balm makes lashes grow fuller and thicker. Hey. At the very worst, you're moisturizing your eyelashes. At the very best, you're getting sexier. And any man who says he doesn't care about having sexy lashes is lying.

A WHAT?

FACIALS

Your face gets dirtier, has larger pores, and more ingrown hairs than a woman's. You're prone to ignore stress from work, and brush it aside when it's generated by family. You irritate your skin shaving and then tend to it cursorily. The result? Men need facials more than women.

Aw, for Pete's sake. No one's going to see you. Or at least no other guy who's going to tell. What's he doing there anyway? Having a mudpack? Could be. You should try it. But later for that.

A good facial, with a low level of abrasion, administered by a skilled technician, can help eliminate blackheads, unruly eyebrows, nose hairs, and especially the occasional freaky hair that pops out of the middle of your face. But then, that's why God made beloveds. Though that's not why he made Gunilla Knutson.

SITES FOR FOUR EYES

CHOOSING GLASSES

Movies have worked the myth more times than Mickey Rooney has played someone short. The duck-faced nerd takes off his glasses, musses up his hair, and suddenly— who'dathunkit?—there stands every dreamboat from William Holden to Superman. But what was so intriguing about the geek in the first place? There must have been some mystery, some promise of surprise radiating from behind those frames—which is exactly what makes eyeglasses extremely sexy.

Considering that the only other facial element you can change without outpatient status is your hair, and that mainstream acceptance of cosmetics for men is about as likely as a k.d. lang voice-over for Burger King, men ought to greet the prospect of wearing glasses as they would the cure for acne, instead of as a corrective for an inadequacy.

Contacts are boring. You don't wind up looking any better than when you couldn't see what you looked like. In designer colors, they are to laugh, unless you want to be taken for Nastassia Kinski's brother in *Cat People*. You can't flip them on, flip them up, toy with them, finger them, bite them, or twirl them.

You can with glasses, though, since they are not only a great accessory but also a great prop. Glasses afford spontaneity. Best of all, because they offer a multitude of changes in persona (sometimes more varied than the wearer's personality), you should develop a wardrobe of them and not just stick to one or two frames.

Unfortunately, most people, including optical specialists, choose classic, textbook frames, which are based solely on complementing facial structure. So, you'll hear that square faces should never wear square frames, round faces should never wear round frames, oval faces have the luxury of wearing anything, and the heart-shaped or triangular faces need something to offset the sharpness of the chin and the lack of a jawline.

Big mistake.

The fault line holding up these guidelines presupposes that all facial elements other than shape are negligible. Yet, if your moon face comes equipped with a big nose, roundness is not the first thing you see in the mirror. Cheekbones (or lack of them) are the source of more vanity than ovality. There is also built-in prejudice, as if something's wrong with a round face, or that you should be embarrassed by a pronounced chin. What if you like the odd things about your face? Why not reverse the premise—celebrate what you've got and balance off what you don't? Glasses should individualize, not make you look like everyone else. All it takes is a little honest perception and assessment.

1. Acknowledge immediately that if you wear glasses and you're meeting others for the first time, the first thing anyone notices about your face is your frames. That's why you should never try to fade glasses into the background. There's no point in denying the obvious. Instead, make people aware that your glasses are your choice.

2. When you buy glasses, push yourself a little further than where you thought you wanted to go, since they reflect the one important feature another person can't readily see—personality. In some ways, it's the most determining of factors.

3. If you can't really see yourself without them, buying eyeglasses is the one time you shouldn't go shopping alone. Or it's an excellent reason to own contacts.

4. Big noses are very cool, and impossible to hide. If you want to offset one, an eyeglass frame with a double bar across the bridge, a keyhole—like the ones found in classic aviators—or a large nosepiece will help. Do not attempt the ruse of pulling your glasses down on your face. It only makes you look sloppy or as if you needed new glasses. In addition, it's important that the nosepiece actually be wide enough so that the glasses don't perch as if sitting out there in space. This will make your nose seem even larger, as if nothing would fit on a bridge that wide. Another stupid people trick is perching the earpieces high on the ears: the I-don't-really-take-wearing-these-glassses-seriously approach. It's an affectation more self-conscious than cute. Glasses should fit close, into your eyes. Own them.

5. Don't compete with a heavy brow line. Choose either frames that come below it or clear frames. If you're buying sunglasses, however, select a pair that occludes the brow. Unlike eyeglasses, sunglasses can eliminate the competition.

6. If your eyes are close and deep-set, don't select clear frames with a heavy nosepiece, no matter how trendy they may be. You need to bring focus away from the center of your face. A detail on the temple side of the glasses is better. Large frames also increase the perception of tiny eyes (unless, once again, you're buying sunglasses). Small frames work best, especially when they fit right into the eye socket.

7. If you don't have cheekbones, avoid frames so narrow they stop above the cheekbone line you don't have. Try frames with strong angles, i.e., rectangular frames with a hard edge, frames that are a little longer on the bottom than the top, which will give you width in relation to your jaw.

8. Classic aviators work well with a triangular face. So would a wee pair of glasses if you decide that you want to have fun and play off a character type.

9.   If you have a really high forehead, it's important *not* to have your glasses happening up there, as the conventional wisdom goes, but from the brow line down. The problem with the standard solution is that it does not break up the forehead as much as it makes you look constantly surprised. The effect is not so pronounced when tried with sunglasses, but then you run the risk of making your head appear four inches taller.

10.   If your hairline is receding, don't try to catch it with big glasses either. Give yourself frames with a strong horizontal line. Crystal frames are a big mistake. They will just make your head look as if it doesn't know where to stop.

11.   Just as a beard changes your type of face, it alters the type of glasses you should wear. In general, the frames need to be smaller and closer to the eye socket. Sunglasses should get smaller too. Stay with the same pre-beard-size frames and you'll probably look like one of the cops in *Serpico*.

12.   There are a few advantages to baldness. One is the ability to wear the most ornamental glasses you like. Knock yourself out.

Once you've found a pair you're happy with, go back and do it again. And again. How can you own only one pair of something so prominent in your wardrobe? This is a line of thinking that adheres to the antiquated notion of glasses as a corrective, like a leg brace. Instead, look at it this way. You don't own just one pair of sunglasses, do you? Well, which do you wear more often? It's no different than buying sweaters, or shoes, or bathing suits. You don't wear them all, but you need them all. Choice is everything.

WHAT'S THAT SMELL?

CHOOSING A SCENT

Perfumers, sniffing a big change in the wind, have new ways of seducing you. Aromatic advertising has always been about fantasy come-ons, but they previously were braced by aging Hardy Boyish naivete—a windbreakered and just slightly leathery paragon, smirking mannishly against the salt spray and the whoop of a tight jib while a barefoot corn-silk beauty waits knee-deep in warm surf, peering at the edge of the horizon; a doe-eyed Polynesian with starling black hair smiles knowingly, half-hidden in the hibiscus.

Gone. That was then. This is Eternity. Slicked back and naked, soaking wet and open-mouthed. Arms folded, hips thrust, with no patience if left untouched, almost angry in anticipation, lean and tattooed, hungry for desire. Pleasure? Maybe, but that's not important. Where are you? I've gotten rid of everyone else. I'm ready. Justify my love.

What brought this on? Sex. And the lack of it. Never has it been so talked about while being so nervewracking to achieve. Why turn your nose up at proven ammunition?

So, banished are the days when cologne was something people gave you on one of those occasions when no one knows what to get you, and you wore it because you knew they would be able to tell if you didn't. Men are splashing on potions in record numbers, in hopes they'll get wet.

The gentlemen's fragrance area in most urban department stores currently stocks around 70 varieties. Its aisles are lousy with essence terrorists. Total sales are approaching $2 billion, with the fastest growth market being young males who made malls their clubhouses, where perfume counters were a great place to meet girls.

Good designers, bad designers, watch companies, car companies, pop stars, romance novel cover boys, opera singers, chefs, athletes—they're all bottling their odors as if theirs don't stink. Can't afford the shearling, make the payments on a Porsche, hit a high D? Buy the deodorant. Buy the shave balm. Buy the eau de toilette, even if you can't pronounce it. But whose? How to decide?

◆ What a surprise. You don't give a crap about knowing patchouli from lavender. In fact, you don't care if Neo-Synephrine is in the bottle as long as it turns someone on. If you have a certain foreign body and soul in mind, one whose smell you can recall even by a coffee machine in a dank hallway, maybe you should bring that person with you, one of the few times, besides when buying eyeglasses, when another person's senses are worth trusting.

◆ If you're using it for bait, however, rely on no one else. Women worry about the message a scent sends out to others. Is this too flowery? Do I smell cheap? Men are content with how something smells as an end in itself. So, in many ways, the cologne picked is far more personal a choice, because it's a source of self-satisfaction.

♦ Know your own scent. Not how you reek after three games of one-on-one and a lawn weeding. Your own smell after your body has been freshly showered and dry for a half hour. A combination of diet and genetics, it is usually overlooked, and yet it is an unignorable factor in cologne selection.

♦ Because of the above, it's impossible to tell how a flavor you like on someone else will smell on you. You must try it on yourself.

♦ At least one third of those scents available at the fragrance counter are in the surrounding air at any given time. When you spray yourself with a tester (on the wrist is best, not that much), walk away to another part of the store, or better yet, outside. Wait about ten minutes, then sniff. If you sprayed so much that you can smell it on yourself without raising your forearm, you don't know how to wear cologne. It's not aftershave. You're not supposed to know it's there unless you check. It's for someone else to detect.

♦ Unfortunately, you can test only a few about-to-linger aromas at a time. After that, what you're smelling doesn't come in one bottle.

♦ You don't have to choose only one. Cultivate a "wardrobe" of fragrances so they can match your moods. Of course, this implies that you are enough in touch with yourself that you know your moods. For that, you may need another book.

- Do your shampoo, shaving balm, deodorant, body lotion, hair tonic have scents too? If any of these have distinctive odors, you need to factor that into your selection. If one of them winds up a saboteur of your prospective new mating call, you may need to switch to an unscented product. The shampoo, not the cologne.

- We're talking water, oil, and extracts here—not steroids, a rowing machine substitute, or a cashmere sweater. You don't get wittier. You don't get tougher. You don't get livelier, unless you swallow a lot. You don't get stiffer. If eau de whatever makes you a little more confident, it's done its job. It can help you wind up. You've got to pitch.

- There is something to be said for no cologne. A whiff of clean, healthy skin—the result of exercise, a healthy diet, a good attitude, and a fresh toothpaste—can be just as much a turn-on. But then you need to have accomplished all those other things. A woman friend's first love was a man who smelled just like fresh-cut pineapple after basketball and sex. To this day, she can't go near a piña colada without feeling faint.

GEEKS BEARING GIFTS

BUYING PRESENTS

Admit it. All those sleigh bells ring-a-linging and chestnuts roasting give you the willies. Instead of being filled with holiday spirit, you walk around as if scheduled for an MRI.

It's not the riding-through-a-wonderland-of-snow part. That's cool. But gift buying is a killer. A minefield of decision making that decrees all happy endings dependent on your taste. Could anything be worse? Sophie had a tough choice, but at least hers was clear-cut—pick a kid. You have to dress *all* of them.

Damned if you do, doomed if you don't. And it's not as if the trauma comes and goes once a year either. Anniversaries and birthdays, graduations and promotions, Valentine's and Mother's Day—greeting one or all of them with open but empty arms is just as wedding-minus-the-garter/convertible-without-a-radio unthinkable. So, unless you've chosen to bake everyone Christmas puddings (hey, sorry we're not closer), you've got to find better stuff to gift wrap.

◆ Though shopping at the last minute does not make it any easier, it's not the inherent flaw in bad gift buyers. The big boo-boo is in not *paying attention* until the last minute. Gift buying is all about tapping one's powers of observation and ability to listen. Naturally, a bottomless checkbook often adds a little zip, but a keen awareness of behavior and passions is the surest way to an I-don't-know-how-to-thank-you-how-did-you-know-I-wanted-this-oh-my-God-I-can't-believe-it-you're-just-the-best kind of response. You're dreaming if you think you can hide behind "it's the thought that counts." Not because it doesn't. It does. Once they open that box, *their* thoughts count, big time.

♦ Before you do anything, *make a list* (about a month before G-day would be perfect) of whomever you have to buy for. Not on the back of an envelope. On a fresh, handy-size pad. Leave sufficient space after each name. The pad is not for doodling, nor should you detach pages or use corners as scratch for figuring your utilities bill, or to wrap deflavored gum. Treat this pad with respect, like a child with a primer, for the data it will soon contain could prove fateful.

♦ For at least the next week, *tune into each future recipient's appearance, habits, manners, reactions, and conversation.* Does he make constant movie references? Does she wear different shoes every day? Is he often going Off-Off Broadway? Does she have a thing about belt buckles? Buying retail? Indian food? Has the idea of the two of you sailing up the Bosporus come up, twice? Do the two of them live for golf? Are they always talking about sex, or books? Is anything pierced? Is everything pierced? You'll be surprised—the clues to choosing an appropriate gift are more obvious than Miss Scarlet in the dining room with a candlestick.

◆ Keep the pad handy, so you can *write down your impressions* ASAP. Don't pretend you're going to remember. You might—probably two months later. But why risk it? How long is this going to take for the time it's going to save? If you have any clue, write down the names of possible stores that might satisfy these proclivities.

◆ *Look for a common ground.* Something they love that you love about them. A way someone wants to look that would make either your pride or something else swell. Art you both appreciate. Something you can do together. If your tastes are completely dissimilar, bite down hard and yield to another's desires. Your ego, even leatherbound, is not high on anyone's wish list.

◆ You have mucho giftos to buy? Work out a budget. Be flexible, but *establish a limit on what you can spend per gift.* When it comes to the loves of your life, however, lose control.

◆ When your first shopping day arrives, don't head out in 10 directions. *Plan the day as you would a good scavenger hunt.* Don't try to cover more than two neighborhoods or indoor malls. Leave plenty of room for serendipity. Oh yeah—*TAKE THE LIST WITH YOU.*

◆ Want to shop faster? *Shop alone.* You won't believe how much quicker it goes, and how less equivocal you are.

◆ *Don't meet anyone for a meal,* because the special of the day is almost certain to come with a generous portion of lost momentum, mixed grilling from the peanut gallery, and half-baked recommendations to places your lunch date's been to so few times that at least two numerals in each address will be innocently but invariably inverted.

◆ Why knowingly cast yourself as an extra in a George Romero film? Avoid the ghoulish hordes. *Know when to shop where.*

—Hit department stores at dinnertime, especially on Saturday and Sunday nights.

—Frequent small stores at lunchtime.

—Go to trendy districts in the A.M., optimally 30 minutes after stores have opened, immediately following the eager warm-up–suited ones who help unlock the doors, but before the brunchettas.

—Always shop when it's raining.

◆ *Check that you have your wallet, checkbook, and credit cards* before leaving each store.

◆ *Never let go of packages while riding public transportation,* not even in a taxi, though you're only dashing into a cash-dispensing Skinner box for "just a minute." Cabbies aren't blind, you know. Are they all crooks? C'mon, are all doctors crooks? Of course not—all.

◆ Unless someone feels about a store the way Hitchcock felt about cool blondes, *shun giving gift certificates.* They're colder than Hitch's heroines, guaranteed to elicit a thanks—but good luck getting a kiss.

◆ If you're a regular at a particular store, call in your marker. *The more personal the service, the less draining the day.*

◆ With the exception of newlyweds and students, *don't be too practical.* What people need is rarely what they want.

◆ *Choose accessories over clothing,* and fit becomes a nonissue. Besides, they're an indulgence, rarely indulged in, and one yard of cashmere costs a lot less than eight.

◆ If you are buying clothing, don't go any which way *but* loose. Unless you know the idiosyncrasies of a designer's sizing, *seek apparel that allows a margin of error,* like full sweaters, draw-string pants, and drapey coats. If you insist on opting for a tailored item or shoes, make sure it's exchangeable.

◆ *Buy the unexchangeable and be ready to wear it or live with it.*

◆ *Don't buy anyone vases, paintings, or tchotchkes unless*

you've been inside their home or gone with them to an appropriate gallery.

♦ *Making a flea market date is one of the best ways to pick up on someone's taste.*

♦ *People make fun of those fruit-of-the-month clubs. Until they're sent the first shipment.* The only problem with biting into a pear, strawberry, or slice of pineapple that tastes exactly like a premium sorbet bearing its name is you get so spoiled, 24-hour supermarkets no longer seem like such a godsend.

♦ *Never hestitate to buy something merely because it looks too cool or too pretty.* Most folk like cool and pretty, especially if they think of themselves as either, definitely if they think of themselves as both.

♦ The best children's book ever written is *Harold and the Purple Crayon* by Crockett Johnson (HarperCollins). You must buy it in hardcover, however. Paperback books make tacky gifts, even to kids.

♦ *Jewelry always scores big*, provided the receiver wears it (men are more receptive when the metal looks tough enough to scar steel). Otherwise, this is not the day to overhaul someone's sartorial nature.

♦ *If a man resents wearing a tie for work, why are you buying him one as a gift?*

- *Smile*, though your feet are aching. Salespeople will treat you like the Second Coming, or at least as good as the Brother from Another Planet. Thank them for being so helpful and they'll offer you lodging.

- In a store it's okay to be selfless. On the way home it's not. *Keep your mind on where you are and what you're doing.* It's not just the grinch that steals Christmas.

- If it's holiday time, *for every 4 gifts you buy them, buy 1 for you.* The cost is sort of buried, it sure brightens the day, and who knows better what you want? Have yourself a merry little Christmas, even if you pay so yourself.

- You'll know *you've bought something exceptional for someone when it hurts to wrap it.*

- *You know you're merely mortal when you decide to keep it and buy them something else.*

HAVE GONE, WILL TRAVEL

A GUIDE IN 5 PARTS

Going away again? Ah, think of those stone bridges, quaint inns, warm fires, lucrative contracts. Nice. Fine. Just remember severe wardrobe edit, indifferent cabbies, dehydration, wrinkled linen, snapshot junkies, foreign customs, U.S. Customs. Don't forget to write.

LEAVING

1. Reservations. Confirmations. Aggravations. Why bother? Find a good travel agent. They know nice hotels. They ask questions you don't until you get there. They know people, make deals, and save money, because it often costs you nothing. That's right, nothing. In case no one's told you, most commissions come from the other side.

2. A travel agent who doesn't get you boarding passes in advance isn't a good travel agent. Next.

3. Renewing a passport is as much fun as visiting the DMV.

Unless you're dying to finish yet another new L. Ron Hubbard novel (how *does* he do it?), there are people who'll endure this for you. They're listed in the Yellow Pages under "Passport & Visa Services." For what it will cost you to wait, it's a bargain.

4.   The 10,000-mile journey to enlightenment starts with a single vaccination. Don't wait until the last minute. Some cause a reaction, and it's no fun to start either a vacation or a quest puking with a rash.

PACKING

5.   Do not do it too far in advance. You won't remember what you put in there and you'll panic.

6.   Garment bags are great if they're going to hang or lie flat. If you're folding and checking, however, you're better off with a regular suitcase.

7.   If you're shopping for new luggage, consider what a bag weighs empty.

8.   When choosing what to pack, consider all options but exercise some logic. You won't need a tuxedo for water rafting. Don't take hiking boots to Venice.

9.   You're going to go through more underwear and socks than you think. And cotton doesn't dry in the room that fast. Pack more undies.

10. Use the Jelly Donut Theory—hard stuff on the outside, squishy stuff on the inside. But line the flat sides of the suitcase with semi-unwrinkleables like sweatclothes, jeans, and socks so protruding heels and hair dryers don't jab when you're lugging.

11. For short or business trips, stick to black or gray, and white, plus one color. Or blue, brown, and white, and no other color.

12. Want to know why some suits cost so much? Pack a cheap one. Pack a better one. You'll see.

13. Most business travelers pack more pants than sport jackets. It's the other way round. You're at meetings. Who sees your pants?

14. Turn your jackets completely inside out.

15. Patterned shirts hide wrinkles better than solids (except solids look neater. Sorry).

16. Don't fold your ties, roll them. Then put them in jacket pockets.

17. Cotton sweaters are more versatile than wool.

18. But cashmere's warm, weightless, and barely takes up room.

19. Take leather. Leave suede home.

20. The most versatile item of sportswear you can pack is black jeans.

21. Interlock your belts around the inside circumference of the suitcase.

22. Do you need that whole bottle of shampoo for five days? Buy plastic bottles and labels. But make sure they're screw-ons, not pop tops.

23. If you're going on a holiday, do you want to be practical, or look incredible? Take as many of your favorite clothes as you can carry.

24. It's also more fun to buy new for where you're going than for when you've come home.

25. Still, leave a small void in one suitcase if you're planning to spree.

26. However, if you act as if foreign currency were printed by Parker Brothers, take along a cheap, empty nylon duffel bag for the return booty.

GOING

27. If you're driving, know how to change a flat. Be affili-
ated with some kind of roadside assistance. Or do you want
to depend on the kindness of strangers these days?

28. Don't hitch a ride. Don't offer one. Not very brotherhood
of man, is it? Yeah, well.

29. No matter how warm the weather, wear your topcoat
onto the plane, then fold it inside out in the overhead. It eats
up too much of the suitcase, and unpacks as if it had been
chewed. Wear your boots on board as well.

30. Our last cab driver proudly admitted he identified the
Statue of Liberty when testing for his license. Too bad you
can't drive there. Don't rely on anyone else for knowing the
quickest way to an airport. Learn an alternate route while
you're at it. When you're out of town, ask the concierge.

31. In New York, the fastest way to La Guardia Airport is
the 59th Street Bridge, lower level, to Northern Boulevard,
until 94th Street. Make a left and follow 94th straight to the
airport. Non-rush-hour Guinness-worthy time: 11 minutes.

32. The fastest way to John F. Kennedy International Airport is usually from another city.

33.   Never let fabulous baggage out of your sight, or bring a clean handkerchief to the luggage carousel.

34.   Your carry-on should contain: all your cash and traveler's checks, checkbook, passport, tickets, jewelry, personal effects, toiletries, reading material, work, gifts (if possible), medicine, house keys, and a change of clothes should the unthinkable happen.

35.   Tags fall off. Paste your name and address *inside* your luggage as well.

36.   It's just an observation, but handlers throw tapestried luggage harder—and don't catch it. Look at it. Can you really blame them?

37.   Some terminals, like TWA at Kennedy, don't sell chewing gum. Stock up.

38.   If you suffer chronic ear agony during descent, talk to your doctor about taking Sudafed.

39.   If you're not going straight to the meeting, why are you wearing your suit on the plane?

40.   If you are going to be sitting in a car, train, or plane for a long time, take your bulky wallet out of your back pocket, even if you know a good chiropractor at your destination.

41. Not the howdy-neighbor type? A Walkman and dark sunglasses for the first half hour of the flight should do it. Just to be sure, balance a Doris Lessing novel on the shared armrest.

42. Traveling without children but sitting next to one? At the first sign of rambunctiousness, either slip the kid a sly, deadly word of warning or complain loudly. Remember, the little charmer didn't pay for his seat.

43. Brought the little googling snookums with you? Change your bundle of joy in the bathroom, where all the bundles belong.

44. Don't touch the almonds.

45. Stewards won't tell you which meal they prefer, so don't ask. Just remember to request the tangerine-mushroom sauce on the side, and if you like your protein intake rare, the only entree they have control over is steak. Lucky you.

46. You're really better off ordering the fruit plate or the vegetarian meal. If you're really hungry, then order the kosher one. Unless it's Passover. Then, you don't want to know.

47. Liquor promotes jet lag.

48. Drink enough water to make you go to the bathroom more times than the kid. If you're in economy, bring your own, because your tongue will feel like the Bonneville Salt Flats by the time someone gets to you.

49. If you're interested, check with a homeopath about ephedra, which inhibits dehydration, reducing jet lag.

50. When they announce descent, go to the bathroom, massage your head, comb your hair, wash your face, moisturize, brush your teeth, change your socks. Let 'em knock. Who cares?

51. Put your boots back on at least a half hour before arrival, unless you're auditioning for *Richard III* as soon as you land.

52. If you're traveling overseas, make sure you've: a) not worn black or dressed as if you've come straight from a Nine Inch Nails concert; b) shaved; c) taken out your earring; d) not rehearsed any witty, smartass remarks should a customs official request you answer those boring routine questions. They won't laugh. Unless they've wiped the stupid grin off your face.

53. If they search your stuff and find nothing, they have to repack it the way they found it. It may take forever, but stand your ground. The revenge is real sweet.

54. Learn how one says "Where's the bathroom?" *before* you get there.

STAYING

55. People who need people are called houseguests. If you're staying longer than four days and your friends don't have a mortgage on the Ponderosa, be a real pal—check in to a hotel.

56. Showing up at friends' with bags but empty-handed is as classy as turning over their dinnerware. Bring a house gift. Anything.

57. If you're in town on business, even for only one night, check in to a hotel. Let the business pay. Let your friends take you to dinner.

58. If you're rich, this is the best time to act like it.

59. Why stay in better hotels? Because they can launder in a few hours. Because they have room service when it's 3 A.M. but your body thinks it's dinnertime. Because they know places you don't. Because they sew buttons, press faster, have clout with maître d's, offer feather pillows, have the electrical adapter you forgot, feed your dog, remember your name.

60. Vacationing cheapskates justify institutional hotels by saying, "How long are we going to be in the room anyway." If it's a memorable vacation, plenty. Treat yourselves right.

61. Don't live out of the suitcases. Stake a claim. Unpack completely as soon as you get into the room. Ask for two dozen hangers. Put your books on the nightstand. Carry framed pictures. Rearrange the furniture if you like. Take a shower for way too long, then use every towel in the bathroom. There're plenty more.

62. Some hostelries won't allow an iron in the room, and the pressing service costs more than a person-to-person call through the hotel operator. Always travel with a steamer. It takes up less room than a shoe.

63. Woe to the media junkie in a far-off land, in a hotel without MTV and CNN. Ask your agent about their availability when you book.

64. If you buy it, and you can't wear it, why schlep it. Ship it.

65. In some countries, belching is considered polite. Go somewhere else.

66. You keep reading about steaks costing over $100 in Tokyo. But why eat steak in Tokyo? The Japanese don't come here for sushi. Let's have a little sense of adventure.

67. Don't eat raw shellfish anywhere. There's adventure, and then there's food poisoning.

68. Telephone service outside North America usually employs pulse dialing. Consequently, you can't phone home for messages. If that's a must, pick up a Tone Dialer—keypad on one side, speaker on the other, producing the necessary tones for message retrieval when pressed up against the mouthpiece—at an electronics store. The gadget is the size of a credit card and shouldn't cost more than $20.

69. A respite is no reason to abandon exercise. In fact, it should be just the opposite. You're supposed to come home looking better than when you left.

70. Outside America, asking what people do for a living on first meeting is right up there with making fun of the faces on their currency. When in Rome, don't be a gladiator.

71. Even inside America, as long as you're away from home, it's not your turf. Be extra nice. Who knows how the locals treat folks they don't like.

72. Excepting cabbies at JFK, everywhere you go someone speaks a little English. But learn key native phrases. It shows respect. It makes a difference. Except in France.

73. Taxis in Eastern European countries clock different rates for different clientele. Pay attention. Check the meter.

74. A second class ticket on a train in Europe or South America is one step above being a passenger on a boatlift.

75. If you're going through more than one roll of film a day, you may be on holiday but everyone with you is in hell.

76. If you're on sort of a second honeymoon, be so ridiculously romantic your partner thinks you're on something.

77. If you're not, note that safe sex is considered a big joke in most of the world. But no one laughs when you mention AIDS. Don't forget. The come-on may be different, but the rules don't change.

RETURNING

78. This is when you wish you were home already. If you are coming back from Western Europe, get to the airport about ninety minutes before your flight. American carriers are not featured as prominently; terminals are more ramshackle; no one will get that worked up or perhaps even comprehend that you're running late; and most important, you have to leave ample time to answer all those questions about the letter bomb you agreed to carry for that Iranian man in exchange for his watching your luggage for a half hour while you went back to your room.

79. If you are coming back from Eastern Europe or the Mideast, get to the airport about two hours ahead. If it's summer, three hours. If you think this is nuts, ask someone who's been there. When you get to an airport like Istanbul's, do not—repeat, do not—get on what appears to be a line. There is no such thing. Those people have been there for days. Just push your way ahead, like the obnoxious Yankee that you are. Use any trick you can to sneak ahead. Does this sound horrible? Do you want to get home?

80. Leave yourself enough currency to buy magazines and

some food at the airport. If you think we have delays state-side, just wait. Because you will.

81. If you buy art, or would like to think it's art, have the dealer write "one of a kind" on the receipt and you won't have to pay duty on it at customs.

82. Otherwise, do you really think you're going to put one over on a customs officer? Most of them can finger a lapel-pulling, receipt-tossing, new-clothes-wearing wiseass faster than a diner waitress can smell burned coffee. If you've gone on a spree and lack an Oscar Madison poker face, scale down the numbers if you've got to, but pay an adjusted duty. It saves so much on reentry anxiety, and you're bound to get a megadose in about an hour.

83. Factor in the last day of your furlough as one that you spend mundanely at home. Unpack, do laundry, look at, but don't answer, mail. Don't call work, don't call friends, and if you've been somewhere really, really restful, don't walk out-side. You'll flinch every time someone brushes your shoulder. Right now, there's no place like home, which is why you wish you were anywhere but here. Reentry's a bitch.

TRAVEL RULE TO LIVE BY #1: Nothing is fun for the whole family unless the parents are under ten.

TRAVEL RULE TO LIVE BY #2: If you want to get away from it all, don't take it all with you.

TRAVEL RULE TO LIVE BY #3: Nobody has towels worth stealing anymore.

BEHAVE

LOOK WHAT YOU LOOK LIKE!

POSTURE AND PRESENTATION

Take your shirt off and get in front of the mirror. Have a good look. C'mon. Don't be a baby. No washboard abs, huh? But were there ever? All right. So maybe the Soloflex guy and you look like different species. But does he have three kids and a lawn that grows clover as if it were a cash crop?

Look, it's obvious. If you don't work out at a gym regularly, you're not going to be approached for the cover of *Joe Weider's Muscle & Fitness*. However, that's not the point of this examination. What you *should* be checking out, what's far more important, is, are you standing the way Mother told you to—shoulders back, chest out, hips square, spine straight, butt in, feet flat, head high, and weight evenly balanced?

Okay. Now we got a problem.

There's only so much a suit—new, custom-made, or costing more than the little one's braces—can do to make you look smart, sharp, and successful if you don't present a staunch foundation to hang that suit on. No one is going to think of you as solid as a rock if you look like you're imploding.

Mom tried to tell you this when you were a slouchy,

slicked-back smartass. Naturally, you thought she was nagging when what she was really doing was acting as both your first personal trainer and motivational speaker (you didn't think Anthony Robbins was born in an attaché case, did you?).

But what did an invincible youth care about aging's natural tendency to droop one's shoulders because it's easier? About how the male's propensity to gain weight fastest in the gut prods a lazy body into caving in from the increased gravity pull? About the way even men who have never had a problem standing straight eventually feel challenged?

Still think you're invincible? God bless you (but what do you do for sex?). As for the rest of you, who have seen the twilight, throwing your shoulders back may not be accomplished so effortlessly, no matter how strong the desire to deny time's passage.

However, correct posture is not merely a stalwart I'll-show-you stance against Father Time or a visually pleasing affectation. Rather, it promotes:

Better breathing

Improved circulation

Mental alertness

Fewer back problems

Stronger vocal projection

Higher sustained levels of energy and endurance

Increased confidence

Focused concentration

Smoother digestion

Healthier-looking skin

Lower doctor bills

Lower shoe repair bills

Less gas

Not bad for something that doesn't cost you a dime. All you have to do is work at it, though not necessarily the way you assume you do.

For achieving good posture has nothing to do with joining a gym, finding a trainer, starting the day with seven hard-boiled eggs, and then working out for two hours four days a week. That's weight lifting—the development of short, squat muscles with limited motion for the sheer power of it. What aids good posture is the growth and flexibility of long, sinewy, supple muscles that can handle the constant repetition of everyday movement.

Frankly, you could accomplish this at a health club, with a trainer. But if you're the type who thinks a heavy bench press is what you do when you're watching a playoff game in over-time, I'll bet you that last bag of nachos, your first day at a busy gym is going to intimidate worse than crashing the last lap of the Indy 500 in a Hyundai.

Then find a quieter, less conspicuous alternative. The good news is you can do this at home. You can do this at work. The bad news is you have to do this or you're going to spend the rest of your life paying the consequences for walking around with your shoulders on top of your ears.

ATTITUDE

◆ The key to acquiring and maintaining good posture is to have a consciousness about it. Life is hard, life is stressful, and too often we walk around reflecting that. Become aware of your movements, such as when you're standing with all your weight on one leg or taking short little breaths that are so common when the rounding of the shoulders constricts the chest. Years of ignoring or accepting these bad habits have weakened these muscles. Tuning into them will help strengthen them.

◆ To remain standing tall, however, will take exercise. Two kinds are necessary. The first is cardiovascular—running, biking, hiking, skiing, or simply walking—three times a week for at least 20 minutes at a time. If you don't think you have the time, talk to someone who's survived a heart attack, or has a pacemaker, and then see how busy you are.

The second form of exercise is stretching. All stretching requires is room for you to lie on the floor (either on a mat or a thick towel on top of the carpet), some discipline, and a minimum of 10 minutes, roughly the time it takes you to go down to the coffee wagon for a cruller you've never enjoyed and a decaf you never finish.

BACK

- The Ultimate There's-No-Excuse-for-Not-Doing-It Back Exercise. Stay seated in your chair but push away from the desk. Spread your legs and plant your feet a little more than shoulder width apart. Bend over and let your body hang. Take slow, count-to-4 breaths, in and out. Do not bob. (Never bob while doing any exercise. You strain muscles, and you're at that age when you can pull something and wind up with a valid and painful excuse to do nothing for weeks.) As you breathe, try to relax and lengthen your arms, your back, and your shoulders. Try this every 2 hours for 30 seconds to a minute.

- Stand with your shoulders back and relaxed, feet flat, shoulder width apart. Raise your arms straight in the air, palms facing each other. Do not look up. Slowly bend to one side as if your body were trying to make the letter C. Hold that position while inhaling and exhaling slowly 4 times. Come up. Bend to the other side. Repeat the breathing. Do 4 repetitions on each side.

- Get on your hands and knees, arms directly under your shoulders, perpendicular to the floor, thighs squarely under the hips, knees on the floor, feet directly behind (sex manuals call this doggie style; there, now you got it). Start with your back flat. Do this sideways in front of a mirror at first if you have to. Exhale completely and arch your back while tucking your chin into your chest. Feel the stretch. Now inhale deeply while you drop your back into a concave position and raise your head up so that you're looking to the sky. In yoga, this is called the cat position (see the difference in perception by those enlightened?). Repeat 4 times. The more slowly you do these exercises at the beginning, the better.

Another sagacious yoga reference. If it doesn't screw up your coordination, try breathing in through the nose and out through the mouth on all cited exercises.

◆ Stand with your feet flat on the floor, slightly more than shoulder width apart. Bend your arms so that your elbows are up and out and your thumbs are on your chest. Inhale, and then as you exhale, slowly twist to each side. Do not yank, fling, or pull. If your back cracks, fine—that's a bonus, not a goal. If not, do not force it until it does. Start doing this 5 times in both directions, then increase to 10.

◆ Lie prone, forearms down on the floor, palms down at your shoulders, pelvis into the mat, legs straight behind you. Lifting from your chest as you inhale, raise your head, neck, and upper torso as you roll back on your spine, slowly, vertebra by vertebra. Avoid pulling your head or neck back. Your range of motion may initially be less than a foot. Whatever. Don't start out trying to be Bart Conner. Contract the muscles in your rear end. Keep breathing. Exhale, and slowly lower yourself down. In yoga, that's called the cobra pose. (Regretfully, there is no catchily named hardcore equivalent.)

Nevertheless, repeat the exercise—this time, however, pushing off gently with your hands as you try to straighten your arms. When you reach maximum height, continue breathing in deep, even breaths, tightening your butt, trying to feel the back stretch. Relax and repeat 2 more times.

STOMACH

♦ The reason why you need to do sit-ups for posture is that muscles in the body work in opposition to each other. The ones on your left side do not push you over because the ones on the right side brace against them. The stomach muscles are the antagonist of the lumbar muscles in the back. Consequently, a stronger stomach will keep you from hurting your back by allowing you to support more body weight upon it.

♦ Most people do sit-ups wrong. Regardless of the name, properly executed reps do not require you to sit all the way up. Hands clasped behind your head are not supposed to assist in raising your upper torso. The former will squander your efforts, working unnecessary back muscles while relaxing, not strengthening, the stomach at the top of the sit-up. The latter makes it too easy to hurt yourself.

♦ So, lie on the floor, flat. Now bend your legs, spread them slightly, and try to keep your feet flat (legs will be bent at slightly more than right angles). Place your hands lightly on your chest or touching your temples. Bring yourself up about 6 inches off the floor, pulling in the stomach muscles as you exhale, as if trying to make them touch your spine. As you inhale, lower your back until your shoulders touch the floor and repeat. Start with 3 sets of 15 and work your way up to 3 sets of 40.

◆ Vacuum your stomach. This is not a cut-rate form of liposuction, but a great way to increase breath control. While you're sitting at your desk, suck in your stomach and exhale as much as you can for as long as you can. Tense your stomach until you feel the constriction. Now slowly breathe in as much as you can and expand as wide as you can. Better move away from the desk to start. Repeat 5 times.

◆ Another habit that would be nice to get into. Try pushing away from the dinner table before you can honestly say "Boy, am I stuffed." Besides sounding *so* attractive, it eventually looks as good as it sounds.

NECK

◆ Nothing is less impressive than a man who stands with a turtle neck. No, not the pullover, but that stance where the head seems too heavy and sort of hangs forward on the neck like one of those plastic dogs that used to bob on the back window ledge of a DeSoto. Many of you are closer to that silhouette than you think. How often do you eat by lifting the fork several inches off the plate and then raising and lowering your face to meet it? Perhaps the simplest neck exercise is to eat as if someone were watching you.

◆ Stand tall. Relax your shoulders. Face forward. Inhale. Then exhale and slowly turn your head to the right as far as it will go without undue strain. Leave it there. Bring it back. Inhale. Then exhale, turning to the left. Bring it back. Inhale. Exhale and drop your head and slowly, with deliberate nonabandon, let it roll around your shoulders, twice in one direction, twice in the other. Keep breathing and take your time. You don't win anything if you go faster.

A NOTE ABOUT YOGA: Yoga is a series of disciplines employing a keen awareness of breathing and stretching, all revolving around the spinal column. Its purpose is to increase the body's suppleness, release energy blocked by stress (of which our diaphragm, or solar plexus, is the prime indicator), and clear the thought processes. It is neither hokey nor weird. You don't have to eat brown rice and dirt. You shouldn't feel ascared of taking a class. No one else will laugh at you, simply because they are trying too hard to do the work themselves. And the better you get at it, the more into your own body you get. Save your self-consciousness for the dance floor. In exchange, you may release a magnetism in your personality you didn't know you had. It sure beats a new tie.

THAT'S ENTERTAINING

HOUSE BY YOU

ENTERTAINING ON YOUR TURF

There's a moment during every successful party when the host surveys the happy tumult all around the room—friends and folks clinking glasses, flicking ashes, gulping canapés, sitting in armchairs or on chair arms, sprawled along the carpet or over the cabinets, giggling, shmoozing, flirting—and realizes everyone is having a fabulous time in this space called home. Simultaneously, two sensations occur. On the outside, a smile of quiet satisfaction turns up the host's lips. On the inside, a little voice keeps repeating only one phrase: *"GET THESE PEOPLE OUT OF MY HOUSE NOW!"*

That voice is going to join you at all your parties, good and bad, and if this is how it rants when things are going well, imagine what it sounds like when your gala is less fun than the time you took the neighbor you feel sorry for ice skating and she failed to mention her lactose intolerance when you brought her a hot chocolate with extra whipped cream.

Though it's a given that throwing any house party approaches self-violation, and that you will never be comfortable at it, sometimes it's your turn. However, if you cut your losses, plan well, and accept some necessary agita, when your guests proclaim your soiree simply a scream, you'll be able to appreciate the irony, thank them for noticing, and keep smiling enigmatically. This time-tested philosophy has led some social historians to believe that the Mona Lisa was painted on her mah-jonng night. Interesting, except nowhere in the portrait do we see bridge mix.

1. Don't invite everyone who knows everyone. You must know some people who've never met each other. If not, postpone the party and see a therapist.

2. Most people's RSVP manners stink. If you haven't heard from them by the time you need to know, call. It's not right, but too bad.

3. If you can afford it, hire help. It doesn't have to be Sir John Gielgud with a hand broom. Anyone with two hands, common sense, a common language, and a good attitude will do. Why be a waiter in your own home?

4. Order too much ice—because if you run out, no matter how soon it comes, it's too late.

5. If you're cooking, have everything you need bought, if not prepped, by the day before. Do the flowers then as well. You shouldn't venture more than two blocks from your house on the designated day.

6. Before you go food shopping, make sure you've gone equipment shopping. Having these items will help:

A great set of knives

A food processor

A juicer

A blender

At least 2 chopping boards and 1 carving board

3 platters that wouldn't look out of place in a road company of *Oliver*

A durable hand mixer and a quality whisk

A sturdy garlic crusher

A full set of mixing bowls

Serving bowls that don't look like mixing bowls

Half a dozen oven mitts (somehow they keep getting lost)

The largest frying pan that fits on your stove

A potato masher

7. Having the following items won't help, because after their initial novelty, they'll sit there looking fabulous and useless, since excellent examples of what they produce are often readily available.

A pasta maker (only masochists and shut-ins make their own tortellini)

A bread maker

An ice cream maker

Whipped cream siphons

Those cute little ice crushers that sound as if they were heaving after the twentieth drink

8.   If you're cooking for a bus tour–load, cook your favorite dishes, not your favorite restaurant dishes. Reproducing a chef's handiwork at home is as draining as explaining the irresistibility of Regis and Kathie Lee to the Yanomami, since your "mentor" operates with a toqued staff eager to do his peeling, blanching, reducing, and glazing. All his complicated necessary ingredients (crème fraîche, demi-glace, reductions) were prepared ahead of time by someone else. You want to make it all from scratch by your little lonesome?

Because a restaurant buys in quantity, you're also going to spend a small fortune buying things you need only a tablespoon of.

Keep it simple, meaning dishes that flourish in bulk preparation—roasts, whole birds, stews, salads, pastas.

9.   Figure 10 people to a bottle of liquor, 6 to a bottle of water, 4 to a bottle of wine.

10.   Figure $1/4$ lb. per person per vegetable.

11.   Figure $1/3$ lb. per person for meat or fish (after boning).

12.   Americans assume cleanliness means freshness. However, if the fish on ice in the market looks clean and tidy, with no blood in the gills, nix it. The one with the bloody gills, loose scales, and clear eyes is the one you want.

13. Most oranges—in fact, most citrus fruits—with no green on their skins have been dyed to match your imagination.

14. Don't examine a melon. Press its belly button—you should smell melon.

15. A great steak isn't bright red. It's brick-red to brown.

16. Raw chicken skin should be pinky-white (chicken skin, remember?), not marigold-yellow.

17. If you have olive oil, garlic, lemon, and pepper, you can make almost anything servable.

18. It's astounding how much sautéing reduces the bulk of any leafy green vegetable, i.e., spinach, watercress, escarole. Buy twice more than you think.

19. Side dishes you need to make half of what you think:
Rice
Kasha
Black beans
Lentils
Lemons and limes
Cabbage

20. Don't peel the skins off potatoes, no matter what the recipe says.

21. Ingredients to add to legumes that take a long time to cook:

Best ingredient—chicken stock instead of water

Second-best ingredient—orange juice

Third-best ingredient—vinegar

Fourth-best ingredient—bacon fat

Smartest thing to do—pour them all in

22. If you don't know how to cook, you can still manage a sit-down dinner. Canvass the premium markets about one week prior to the party, purchase ¼-lb. portions of all the prepared foods that intrigue you, take them home, invite someone over, and taste 'em all. There are, however, several food groups to avoid:

Fish—unless you want to serve it cold.

Meats grilled or broiled plain. They never maintain their succulence during takeout.

Within a half hour of arrival, pasta feels like a model's hair after five back-to-back runway shows.

Cooked seafood tastes like vinyl ten minutes after the pasta congeals.

23. That leaves you with stews like osso buco, gumbo, pot-au-feu, and feijoada; almost all roasted fowl (order them slightly undercooked, with some of the pan juices; this way, the purveyor has to make them fresh and you can reheat them to proper doneness—350 degrees is the magic number for immolating birds); rice dishes like paella, grains like orzo, couscous, barley, beans, and lentils; salads; self-contained appetizers like pierogi and spring rolls; marinated seafood like ceviche; any dish with potatoes; roasted root vegetables; mushrooms; and almost every dessert except baked Alaska (unless you're ballsy enough to fake it with, no fooling, a blowtorch).

Note: If you have a reputable butcher who prepares cooked meats, generally order the main course from him rather than from a gourmet shop.

24. However, the neatest way for a noncook to have a truly gosh-old-man-you-did-it dinner party is to cook the main course yourself. Now, before stressing back that facial tick, the secret of all great cooks is knowing that main courses offer the easiest possibilities. If you buy the best meats, fowl, fish, and game, just get out of their way. You can't mess these up. Keep saying that to yourself. You can't mess these up.

Example 1—Steak. A top sirloin 1½ inches thick. Heat a cast-iron skillet until it could melt your school ring. Rub the steak with salt, pepper, garlic, and olive oil to taste. Sear (blacken) it for a minute and a half on one side. Turn down the heat halfway, then cook it on the other side for ten minutes, for medium rare. That's it. It's not about cooking. It's about watching a timer.

Example 2—Duck. Order it fresh from the butcher. Have him clean it and prep it. If he won't do the latter, merely rub salt, pepper, and rosemary inside and out of Daffy. Don't worry how much; it will burn off. Put the bird on a raised rack in a pan and place in an oven at 450 degrees. In 30 minutes, reduce to 350, drain pan, turn bird. In 30 minutes, drain pan and turn bird. In another 30 minutes, drain pan and take out bird. Done. The problem with duck is not that it's fatty. It's that no one wants to stand there and turn the damn thing. Same with goose. Chicken's even easier. It's done about 20 minutes faster and you don't ever have to turn it. But you should rub garlic all around it too.

Example 3—Lobsters. Drop them in salted and lemoned boiling water for 12 minutes. They scream, they die, they're ready. Not so hard, is it? Think restaurants have been ripping you off? You should.

25.   It sounds Mrs. Cleaveresque, but it really is your responsibility to greet everyone and introduce them to each other. You may feel like a schmuck, but your friends will be grateful, especially the 50 percent who've already met 60 times and couldn't remember each other's names if you threatened the lives of their Jeep Grand Cherokee dealers.

26. Always have on music, even if it's not a danceathon. Keep it on low, for the buzz.

27. When there are:

10 guests—they blow the smoke up and look for an ashtray.

30 guests—they puff away and snuff it out in a highball.

75 guests—they flick ashes on the rug and slam the stub into uneaten crème brulée.

Oh, no, not my friends, huh? Betcha don't figure out whodunits till the last reel either.

28. Don't be afraid to ask who the designated drivers are. If no one comes forth, ask for volunteers. If you get none, collect keys.

29. Though vultures could probably learn a thing or two from your brood, should you have mucho leftovers, find out the phone number of the nearest soup kitchen or shelter. You may be surprised how close one is. Make arrangements to either drop the food off or have it picked up.

ENTERTAINING FOR TWO

Follow any or all of the above-cited cooking suggestions. Have the music a little cooler but more prominent. Go easy on the ice. Still collect the car keys. Add a fireplace. If you don't have one, substitute at least one of the following movies with memorably sensual food scenes:

Tom Jones—the meat-gnawing seduction

The Exterminating Angel—the dinner that won't end

La Grande Bouffe—the dinner with a definite end

The Great Race—the pie fight (it depends)

Like Water for Chocolate—what gets on her apron

The French Connection—Popeye Doyle's alfresco dinner

Dinner at Eight—the aspic

The Gold Rush—the soleful meal

Five Easy Pieces—tuna fish between the knees

Last Tango in Paris—the higher-priced spread

Funny Girl—Fanny discovers pâté

The Night Porter—glass-and-jam sandwiches

The Age of Innocence—overhead dinner shots

The Attack of the Killer Tomatoes—credits and first ten minutes

And the best movie about one of the greatest loves of all, *Babette's Feast*

Should luck, skill, fire, and Blockbuster fail you, do not despair. There are four surefire saves:

1. Pour great champagne on the appetizer. Drink the rest.

2. Shmear Sevruga over the entree.

3. Keep scooping vanilla Häagen-Dazs on the dessert. Spill some all over yourself.

4. Have on a sexy pair of great boxers, and try to look modest.

MI CASA, UNLESS YOU TRIP, FALL, AND SUE MI CASA

PARTYING ON THEIR TURF

Don't go to the fridge without asking, stop playing with the remote, stay out of the medicine cabinet (though you won't), use a napkin, no way are you sitting around in sweat-clothes, wait until everyone is served, if you don't help wash you're going to get dished, and remember that none of these people are obliged to drive you anywhere. Otherwise, make yourself at home.

1. You may rationalize, Oh, come on, it's a party, but to your waistline and liver, it's just another four hours. The brain will make concessions. They won't.

2. Food is not less fattening when eaten standing up.

3. Finger food—sitting on puff pastry, wrapped in bacon, filled with cheese and bread crumbs—is rarely lean, just mean. Have something nourishing and filling like soup before you venture out. It'll slow the alcohol, fill you up, and make you less inclined to taste things you'd normally pass up if they were listed on a menu beside a price.

4. Sampling everything on the buffet table is really cool for your system. Why not have a different liquor with each one? Do it up right.

5. If you exercise regularly at night, change your habits during high party seasons. Too many invites right after work. What are you going to bench press after three sea breezes? And if you're thinking of spending the holidays (usually coinciding with, and the initial spark of, high party seasons) someplace warm, you're going to arrive wherever ticked off for feeling flabbily self-conscious. And rightly so. It's bad enough you're pale.

6. House parties are a perfect time to look around for an inspiration if you are still stuck about what to buy the host for Christmas.

7. If the occasion is a sit-down dinner, don't bring a gift that could be construed as a course, like a pie or a cake or a roast, unless you've checked this out with the host before. Many a gourmand takes offense at unexpected menu additions, especially homemade ones. Wine, chocolates, flowers, books are safer tokens of appreciation. And don't you take offense if they don't drink your wine at dinner. If you really liked what you brought, you should have bought one for yourself.

8. Never leave your keys in a checked coat, and certainly never one that's thrown on the bed.

9. Your boss is always your boss, even at a party, no matter what your new best friend says now. Best friends can't fire each other in the morning. And "Boy, was I drunk last night" doesn't work here either.

SIX ON THE BEACH

HOSTING WITH A TAN LINE

Is it the mountain air, the salt spray, or the side effects of Solarcaine? Something about summertime induces 17 percent of the population to suit up in butcher aprons embroidered with elbow jabbers like "I'd like to toast your buns," and the remaining 83 percent into insatiable hunger pangs. Entertaining and sunshine could be a better match than you are likely to make this summer.

Nevertheless, you would think this one season when so much hangs out while hanging out would stimulate communal bulimia. Sadly, friends and family usually attain optimal tan-ready skinniness around mid-June, only to backslide guiltily through Labor Day, as they have "just a sliver," plead for "no more than a half of a half," magnanimously beseech young and old alike to raise their forks "because all I need is a taste"—of anything passing through the kitchen that's organic, inert, and able to fit on Fiestaware.

Gluttony, however, is not the only reason dining under sunblock requires different rhythms than entertaining from an urban half-kitchen. With the allocation of more space, time, mouths, allergies, dietary idiosyncrasies and distractions, weekend or vacation cooks are required to be adaptable, ecumenical, economical, punctual, inspirational, convivial, and knowledgeable about how to start a grill, simultaneously. All this, while finding it necessary to take your clothes off without anyone offering to have sex.

Unless you like ending August as a whiter shade of pale, you need shortcuts.

The following list takes into account common seasonal predilections for grilling, seafood, exercise, experimentation, money pooling, mind altering, sun-blocked intentions, house sharing, mai-tied-one-on laziness, and yours. The hope is to make you a better cook, a better host, a better housemate, and to avoid your spending next year alone under a lean-to in the Seychelles.

1.   The best summer meals are those that employ minimum cutlery, incorporate the cuts of meat with the largest number of big bones, get by on the sparest ladles of sauce, start with the most copious drenching in marinade, consistently utilize the freshest bunches of ingredients, have platefuls of stuff you can twirl and slurp, and are presented with the least amount of heat brought to the table. A successful summer

meal should make you feel either six pounds lighter or eight years old.

2. Wow. Look how many items have a label that screams FAT FREE. Too bad none of those labels have been slapped on you. That's because there's a big difference between a defatted food product serenely isolated inside a jar and that product inside a body.

Why? Read the ingredients. The average we-can-eat-all-we-want-post-barbecued-skinless-free-range-chicken-breast frozen dessert has, on the average, five different kinds of sugar in it.

Why? How come so many variations? Because contents are listed in order of importance, and by eliminating the spread-the-wealth ruse that amalgamates dextrose, fructose, glucose, corn syrup, maple syrup, honey, and malt, the consumer might discover that sugar is the main ingredient in most of these goodies.

And while you may enjoy a sugar rush as much as the next guy, your body can handle only so many of them a day, regardless of your youth dew freshness and hyperurban metabolism. Which means, whatever sugar your body doesn't use, it stores—as fat. The more sugar you use, the more potential fat-in-waiting. As an added bonus, the more sugar crashes you endure, the more potential increased sugar intake you need to overcome them—the even more sugar-in-weighting.

So, unless your dessert can claim fat begone and sugar riddance (often achieved by a pharmaceutical mélange of chemicals lab mice will pay us back for one day), there is no such thing as a free munch.

3.   Think abs.

4.   Nothing wrecks the velvet bristle of a margarita made with a superior tequila such as Sauza Conmemorativo or Tres Generaciones like table salt. The dubious art of Diamond Crystal-ing the rim of a glass is as useless a procedure as tying the perfect bow tie. Why are you bothering? Please do not write letters. This is not a debate.

5.   Furthermore, any man who still thinks his dinner jacket looks jauntiest with a bow tie probably does so because it matches his lucky cummerbund. Nothing like being cinched, pinched, and knotted when you're supposed to be looking your best. Won't you look fresh at the next gala on a hot summer night under a tent. Boy, what you need is a drink. How about a margarita? Straight up. No salt.

6.   Women, want to make men envious, and even hornier than they already are during a heat wave? Don't wear stockings, not even for dinner.

7.   For a picnic, load up the car with everything you need: deck chairs, boom box, hammock, baseball gloves, little white gloves, love gloves. In fact, try not to leave room in the trunk for the food. An enclosed cargo area acts like a large, uncontrollable crock pot, stewing all it encases. If there's room, put the food in the backseat, where it can enjoy the air-conditioned climate comfort food so richly deserves. If there isn't, put the kids in the trunk (though they might go on Ricki Lake) or let them take public transport.

8. There is a period of about two hours when fish goes bad before it starts to smell. You won't be able to spot it. Your body will, but only too late. At a buffet, a picnic, or anywhere food is left on a table for an extended period, serve all fresh fish cold. Refrigerate it as soon as it is cooked and cooled. Pack in ice for the trip. Save your famous braided ragout of bass and monkfish for Thanksgiving. Served then, your guests will think it's an *hommage* to the coiffures of Native Americans and praise your creativity instead of puking their guts up under an August moon in Settler's Brook.

9. Despite its being the most deliriously romantic cooking scene in the history of film, Alvy Singer could have won Annie Hall's heart even faster if he'd known the best way to prepare a lobster. The boiling-it-to-kill-it part he got right—actually he got it wrong, but he had the idea—but after the lobster has silently screamed its way to a watery death in about 60 seconds, take the redcoat out of its liquid chamber and place it on a char-ready grill, 6 minutes on each side. Split the scarlet devil, and if there's roe to be had, whisk it into some scalded butter. That's the deal. Wash down with champagne on ice (you heard me) and no one will ever leave you for a macro ashram.

10. Think abs.

11. You want to throw a party where the gang gets more polluted than the Italian Riviera but can't afford the nonsense of a full bar (how long has that three-quarters-full bottle of Three Feathers from the last soiree because that was your Cousin Manny's favorite, God rest, been sitting in the closet?).

Here's your bar. Water, club soda, beer, cola and diet cola, and a punch made with four white liquors (rum, vodka, tequila, gin) and the citrus fruit drink of your choice. Throw in some grenadine if you like. Throw in some powdered drink mix too, or supermarket sherbet (the no-name-brand half gallon that comes in *X-Files* colors), just for sweetness and to get the stuff racing through the system.

12. An hour before the party is over, 86 the punch. Have the name of three reputable car services handy. Have the kids deliver the left-behind cars the following day. The kid will love you so for the chance to drive a big car.

13. Just because you're outside eating, doesn't mean your cigarette smoke isn't annoying someone else. Deal with it.

14. If you are leaving a barbecue untended before the fire is fully out, pour whole milk on it. It'll make a mess, but at least it's easier to clean up than the aftermath of four-alarm fire.

15. If someone spills red wine on your pretty white linen, pour white wine on it immediately to dilute it. Then club soda. Then wash or clean before it dries.

16. The best part about sharing a house with others is spending their money on food. Portobello mushrooms and white truffles don't seem nearly as expensive when the cost is split 10 ways. If you think your housemates are getting suspicious about your escalating shopping receipts, scale back on mundane things—like ketchup, mayo, soap, toilet paper.

17. Since your famished audience thinks it all happens by magic, get ready for more appreciation than cooperation. Forget about the noncooks who promise, "Don't worry. I'll help." Usually, it's three peeled potatoes and they're out the door with a "let me know when you want me to set the table."

18. If you weekend along beachfronts chronicled on *The Gossip Show* or up hillsides where Saab 900 convertibles in malachite outnumber Plymouth Voyagers 3 to 1, you are undoubtedly an only-game-in-town grocer's sitting duck. Therefore, leave the city a little earlier, stop en route and shop. Produce from roadside farm stands, local fish hatcheries, and sometimes even enlightened suburban supermarkets is cheaper and no less fresh than what's meticulously arranged in pinwheels on marble counters at porcelain-tiled, halogen-lit gougetoriums.

19. To ensure more money for bluepoint oysters and baby veal (oh, boohoo yourself), buy staples—like paper towels, bottled water, Diet Coke, all-purpose flour, Lemon X, olive oil, bleach, Bounce, chewing gum—in bulk at the beginning of the season from discount palaces like Channel and Home Depot.

20. Weekly purchases of fresh herbs throw budgets out of whack. Meanwhile, they're as easy to grow as weeds. When it's still too chilly for splendor in the grass, get thee to a nursery, buy potting soil, small plants of rosemary, thyme, basil, columbine, and other herbs you love, toss them into a few clay receptacles, douse them, Miracle-Gro them twice a month, pinch them back a few times, and you'll be saving bunches by the end of July. (You probably won't have to do this alone. Every house, almost without fail, yields a currently dormant Martha Stewart, who will show up one morning with garden gloves on. Don't waste time trying to sniff out who it might be, however. There will be no prior clues.)

21.   Make the effort to exercise in the morning. Why not look better on the beach than after the fact? And, face it, how motivated are you going to be after a day of sun and/or two pitchers of guava daiquiris when you know you have dinner for 10 to prepare?

22.   Face a complicated recipe on a beach day, and curse your life. (Should you live with cheapskates, they're going to curse your receipts.) Prepare dishes that can simmer for hours. Not only do they taste better, keep longer, taste better after they've been kept longer, don't require attentive tan-time-robbing babysitting, but they clean up faster and are easier to serve.

23.   Aesthetically pleasing though it may be, deveining shrimp is a waste of time. The brown stringy gook under their outside circumference is not pretty, but it's unjust cause for comparisons with Divine. The stuff won't hurt you. (To those nutritional purists who balk, however, answer this one: What are you eating shrimp for in the first place?)

Besides, shrimp taste markedly better when cooked in their shells. Let your guests peel 'em. They didn't help. They're not paying. They might as well do something.

24. Try a splash of vinegar on fish that is marinating.

25. Add fresh grapefruit juice to meats that are marinating.

26. Don't trim all the fat off meat you're going to grill. Do that after the grilling.

27. Fish grills faster than you think. (Ten minutes an inch, total, both sides.) Do not walk away. If you must flirt, do it over the charcoal. Use the smoke for effect.

28. Anyone eating mashed potatoes can't honestly be worrying about stepping on a scale. So to make them taste even better, pour the fat off any poultry you're cooking and into the mush. Even better, fry up all the skin, drain it, dry it, chop it up, and toss it in. Don't you dare bring margarine anywhere near a spud.

29. You can throw almost any fruit or sorbet into a blender with liquor and ice, and people will drink it. (If they're on the beach, the stupider the drink the better.)

30. When served slightly chilled, light red wines like Brouilly or Mouton Cadet are great with grilled meats and fowl.

31. No matter what pie you slave over, no matter how well you perfect your soufflé, the best summer dessert in the history of the universe is ICE BOX CAKE. If you disagree, you don't deserve to eat it.

It's made with Nabisco—and *only* Nabisco—Chocolate Wafers and very sweet whipped cream. The classic recipe is on the box, but since millions believed Lestoil could make water wetter, here is an improved version.

a. First, you must find the wafers. For those of you who grew up in economically upscale but culturally depressed neighborhoods—where you were fooled into thinking Oreos were better than Hydrox (I'd be kicking myself for all those lost years if I were you), and that other kids played skully with bottlecaps because they couldn't afford marbles—you may not recognize the box. It's 1 two-inch-in-diameter cookie high, 1 cookie wide, long, lean, yellow and brown, with a cellophane window in order to check out the ensembled disks for cracks and chips. There are no substitutes. If you can't locate them, it's over. You will get about 7 servings per box.

b. Make whipped cream with more vanilla and a lot more sugar than usual. Stop wailing about how unhealthy this is. Why the hell do you think it's called junk food? (In case you've never made whipped cream: Take ice-cold heavy cream and pour it into an ice-cold metal or glass bowl. Whip with a whisk if you have good forearms, or a mixer if you've paid your monthly utilities. When the cream starts to thicken, add vanilla and sugar to taste—about 2 tablespoons of the former and ¼ cup of the latter per pint. Keep mixing until smooth peaks form, or poking with your finger makes a permanent dent, then stop or you'll wind up with butter. For Ice Box Cake, figure on at least doubling the additions and using about 1 pint of cream per box of cookies. To repeat, there are *no* substitutes. Try Cool Whip or Reddi Wip, and risk being beaten mercilessly by an Ice Box Cake lover if caught. Should the jury be aficionados as well, your attacker will walk.)

c. On a flat try, cookie sheet, or baking dish, line up rows of cookie sandwiches made by scooping a generous schlag of whipped cream and pressing it between two wafers. When you have the cream-pasted cookies all lined up in neat rows, cover the entire thing with more whipped cream. Then take any remaining broken cookies, throw them in the food processor, grind them to dust, and sprinkle the contents all over the top. Refrigerate for at least 24 hours, but 36 is even better if you can keep everyone's paws off it, because then it really turns into cheesy, irresistible devil's food. Serve and gloat.

32. The Cookbooks of Summer:

The Way to Cook by Julia Child (Knopf)

The New York Cookbook by Molly O'Neill (Workman)

Secret Ingredients by Michael Roberts (Bantam)

Fresh from the Freezer by Michael Roberts (Morrow)

The Greens Cookbook by Deborah Madison and Edward Brown (Bantam)

City Cuisine by Mary Sue Milliken and Susan Feniger (Morrow)

The Silver Palate Cookbook by Julee Rosso and Sheila Lukins (Workman)

The Classic Italian Cookbook by Marcella Hazan (Knopf)

Bistro Cooking by Patricia Wells (Workman)

The New York Times 60-Minute Gourmet by Pierre Franey (Times Books/Random House)

From My Mother's Kitchen by Mimi Sheraton (out of print but worth the search)

Bradley Ogden's Breakfast, Lunch and Dinner (Random House)

Feasts by Leslie Newman (HarperCollins)

Square Meals by Jane and Michael Stern (Knopf)

The Manhattan Chili Co. Southwest-American Cookbook by Michael McLaughlin (Crown)

33. Best House Rule Ever Made: Whoever cooks doesn't clean.

34. Old Wives' Tales That Don't Hold True: You *should* put tomatoes in the fridge. You should put bananas in. They keep longer, they taste better. Banana growers started the leave-out-to-ripen ruse because they knew the yellow crescents would turn brown and ugly faster.

35. Best Old Wives' Tale That Holds Up: Remember your mom telling you that you had to wait an hour after eating before you went into the water? Of course you can go in the water right after you've eaten. Because nothing's going to happen. Absolutely nothing. Do you know how attractive your stomach is going to look like after a big lunch? Cramping is not the problem. Lack of crunching is.

36. Think abs. Reckon this is obsessing? See if you feel otherwise after the sun goes down, and still absolutely nothing has happened.

BECOMING A VIP AT FAVORITE RESTAURANTS

LA VOIX HUMAINE QUI A TRÈS FAIM

(Translation: Aren't You Hungry?)

A Play in One Desperate Act

RESTAURANT
OPERATOR: 161-29. Can you hold, please?
   (Minute-and-a-half wait time)

O: 161-29. Thank you for holding. How can I help you?

CUSTOMER: I'd like to make a reservation.

O: Reservations? Could you hold, please?
   (Three-minute wait time)

O: 161-29. Reservations. How can I help you?

C: Yes. I'd like to make one.

O: For what date, sir?

C: Tonight. I know, I know it's asking for a miracle, but I figured, Hey, what the hell. What have I got—

O: Could you hold, please?

(Fifteen-second wait time)

O: 161-29. Thank you for holding. This evening, what I have available is 6:15.

C: Does anyone with their own teeth really eat that early?

O: *(Silence)*

C: Aw, c'mon. There's got to be a cancellation.

O: It's what I have, sir.

C: Jeez. Well, is it in the front room or the back?

O: The bar.

C: The bar what?

O: I have space available at the bar. Do you prefer stools or a high table?

C: Let's skip to the weekend. What do you got Friday?

O: Which Friday, sir?

C: *This* Friday.

O: Could you hold, please?
      (One-minute hold)

O: 161-29. Thank you for holding. My first available Friday
      is September 1.

C: Ma'am, that's Labor Day weekend.

O: Are you not planning on staying in town, sir?

C: I guess we can leave later. For two at 7:30.

O: At 7:30, I have a table available in our expanded Coat
      Check Lounge, or I do see an opening in the rear dining
      room at 11:35.

C: I don't want to come in for a nightcap.

O: It's my only table, sir.

C: All right. You win. Anything to end this. Just don't tell
      me I'm in Smoking.

o: We *never* allow smoking in the Coat Check Lounge, sir, for obvious reasons.

c: No, I mean at 11:35.

o: I'm sorry. Yes, sir. That's two, no smoking, at 11:35. Please note that after 11 we switch to our late-night menu, featuring dishes exclusively from our Blue Mountain hickory grill, or fettunta sandwiches.

c: Can I ask you something, out of curiosity, nothing more? When is *anything* available at a reasonable hour?

o: Will you also be in town Columbus Day weekend? *(Silence)* September 1?

c: The 1st.

o: Can I have both daytime and evening phone numbers?

c: It's the same, 555-8688. 212.

o: And a number in case of emergency?

c: You mean like next of kin?

o: Just a precaution, sir.

c: 555-2373. Should it be necessary, they have a copy of my living will.

O: Please remember to confirm with us 24 hours in advance, no later than 4 P.M. that afternoon. Failure to do so will automatically release your table, and God knows when you'll get in again. Looking forward to seeing you. Thanks for calling 161-29.

fin

Attempt entrée into the restaurant du moment unprepared and you'll wind up contemplating laying siege to a free-range chicken farm. Suddenly you long for one of the 52-pick-up strewn Wokkin' All Nite Long #34 menus that lie wall-to-wall in your vestibule. You stare forlornly into the chilling abyss in your kitchen, at proof of your rotten bring-home-the-bacon habits, trying to pretend a peanut butter–and–mayonnaise omelet might not be so bad, cursing yourself for always looking past the maître d' to see what he is eating rather than listening to his name. You wish you weren't starving. You wish she weren't waiting. You wish you didn't have to jump through hoops for a meal.

You should be put to bed without any supper for thinking that you do.

However, unless you think there's cachet in becoming the local coffee shop connoisseur (isn't one Jane and Michael Stern enough for any hemisphere?), what you must do is take the necessary steps to become a restaurant regular.

Urban life is a little more urbane if your name and silhouette are immediately recognized at a minimum of *three* eateries. Such clout saves time, reduces stress, strokes the ego, impresses business associates, dazzles relatives, and avoids dishpan hands. It's really not that hard to pull off. You're not required to be a magazine editor or an information highway executive, or to start sitting at the same bar night after night like the losers at Cheers. It's not imperative to overextend until you witness a waiter gleefully slicing your American Express card in half. And it's a myth that it takes peeling off $20s like Grandpa loading up a minivanful of his descendants. All you have to be is quick, vocal, sporadically literate, polite, and charming. Now you know why coffee shops are packed.

1.   Most-favored-nation status is not necessarily harder to achieve at established restaurants than at new ones, though the technique is a little different.

The trick to the latter is getting there before the parade passes by. Don't be a wuss and wait for the reviews. Go as soon as you hear the faintest six-winged buzz. At worst, it winds up another bad meal. At best, smart management mentally photoengraves whoever comes before judgment.

As for the former, a canny restaurateur, like a seasoned Casanova, never takes a virgin for granted. And though it's his or her goal to win everyone over, don't play hard to get. It's more advantageous to embrace an arms-outstretched, take-me attitude than an arms-folded, show-me one. Let yourself be seduced.

2.   Once you've discovered a restaurant that has you in thrall, begin by going there for lunch no later than 12:15, before the daily madness begins. Lunch is a shorter shift than dinner, usually involving only one seating, so the house focuses more intensely on the guests. If you can't make lunch, and if they're open, try either an early dinner Sunday or Monday (unless it's one of those ornithic perchings with such a deal for those who love to catch the worm, in which case this chapter is inapplicable. Try showing the host pictures of your grandchildren instead; otherwise, you're on your own) *or* dining after 9:30 (10:30 in New York). Whatever day you select, however, it's wise not to make your maiden voyage during peak hours.

3. When you call to make the reservation, don't lose your cool (provided you encounter no rudeness—if you do, hang up and find another to stir with love). It's not the reservations staff's fault the lines are jammed, and they need a hard time from you like they need a bath in veal stock. Announce your name at the top of the conversation: "Hi, this is Mr. Rubenstein . . ." If your name is odd, so much the better. If not, at least when the reservation is taken, you get to say it again. Repetition counts. But more important, find out the reservations person's name, immediately put it in your Wizard or Newton or under a magnet on the fridge, and don't forget it. Use it each time you call. Make a phone mate.

4. When you finally arrive, remember: manners and eye contact.

5. Waiters are not conveyor belts with wine openers. They are your conduit to this joint. Treat them like dirt and word will spread through the room quicker than what's being 86'd. Restaurants keep lists of preferred customers. Reservations books are annotated. When management wants to know who's been naughty or nice, they ask. And waiters tell.

6.   If you enjoy your dinner and your environment, don't be so cool. Let the house know. If it's not too busy, ask to meet the chef. Shake the waiter's hand. Tip 20 percent. Make it a point to tell the maître d' when you leave. It is also the perfect time to introduce yourself and start a conversation. When you're responsible for 200 people having a good time every night, small pleasantries are greeted like bouquets tossed at an aging diva.

7.   Then, go to the restaurant at least once a week for the first month, twice a month thereafter for the next four months. Start venturing into prime time. You'll see, it's easier. Ever wonder why some people walk in at the height of the rush and are seated immediately? A smart house keeps 15 percent of its tables unreserved even at peak hours for regulars who arrive unannounced. You think it's unfair? In any other endeavor, giving steady clients preference is considered smart business thinking. You're just jealous.

8.   A letter to the editor or a customer service representative often evokes a surprisingly attentive response. You cannot believe, however, the power of the printed word in a food establishment. One damning epistle can have the staff wringing its aprons. A psalm of praise speeds your way into dining Valhalla as if it were a shopping bag full of saffron. Pick up your pen and see how much perkier things get the next time you pick up their flatware.

9.   Think any of this sounds too corny or contrived for someone at your level of sophistication? Too bad, because this is how it works, as surely as cream sauce is the devil's Novocain. If you insist on remaining the strong, silent type, make sure your ass knows how to get real comfy on a barstool. And bring something to read while you wait for recognition. Something by Tolstoy. Like his collected works.

10. On the other hand, don't ever forget: no one is doing you any favors. There are thousands of fooderies salivating for your business. No matter how much fabulosity a bistro seems to exude, it's about a meal. And bad manners should never be factored into the price you pay. Food will always be a hungry buyer's market. So wherever you eat here, don't get gas.

S'ONEDERFUL

IT'S NOT THE LONELIEST NUMBER

Almost everything one's ever read, watched, heard, smelled—each ad that coerced and cajoled, the songs that excited or consoled, movies cried over, TV laughed at, theater cheered for, weddings, births, deaths, the prayers of parents, the best wishes of relatives, the advice of friends, jeez, even one's own daydreams—has been conditioning for that ultimate quest: finding the perfect other one; that soul mate who's somewhere out there, waiting to make you feel brand-new.

Too bad nothing ever prepares one to do something one often does for a good portion of one's life—be alone.

Oh, it comes up in all those tunes and tales all the time, though not in any way enlightening or instructive. Instead, being a sole occupant is delegated as the holding pattern, that in-between stage, time spent testing the waters, as if one's life had not yet taken flight, deserved a spotlight, or been thrown into the deep end.

Not surprisingly, advice on long-range existence in oneness is almost nonexistent, unless one considers cheery titles like *I'm Dysfunctional, You're Dysfunctional* (by Wendy

Kaminer, Addison-Wesley, 1992) inspirational. That's because coping is all that's expected. If one's stuff is found on both sides of the medicine cabinet, forget about thriving. Perish any thoughts of ever being happy. Aren't you nobody till somebody loves you?

Evidently, enough ensembles think so, or else why would unattacheds have to endure the same excuse plied whenever the former explain the perpetuation of their bad relationships? "Well, it's better than being alone."

No. It's better than swallowing a fork, but being alone could be pretty great if you weren't so bad at it.

25 PLUSES ABOUT BEING A SOLE MATE

1. Sitting anywhere you want at the movies

2. Reading, even while you eat

3. The remote

4. Vacuuming naked

5. Dancing around the apartment (you do too)

6. Making a mess when you're real late

7. Picking your nose during the climax of *Masterpiece Theatre*

8. Finding everything just where you left it

9. Ordering liver in a restaurant without anyone at the table going "Ugh"

10. Getting to play the Grateful Dead, Jethro Tull, Sheena Easton, and KC & the Sunshine Band without begging

11. Seeing something you like in a store, going to another to compare the price, then returning to the first one to buy it, with no complaints of "Why can't you do that tomorrow?"

12. Leaving when you want to

13. Serendipity

14. No voice pleading "Come to bed, honey" when you're wide-awake, then having that certain someone fall asleep on your arm

15. Eating fettuccine at home with your fingers

16. Farting without pretending nothing happened

17. Singing in the car so loudly that the car in the next lane applauds

18. Pornography (much better when you're on your own, so to speak)

19. Not having to readjust the driver's seat or rearview mirror

20. A drastic reduction in the number of invitations to children's birthday parties

21. A little self-reliance, perhaps?

22. Whizzing in the shower (those bodily freedoms do add up)

23. Exotic hair experiments with mousse

24. Talking to yourself

25. A pet's undivided and unequivocal love

THE ONE ACT A SOLEMATE SHOULD NEVER COMMIT

Purchasing any item boasting a label like CAMPBELL'S SOUP FOR ONE. Only women in Stephen King novels do that.

GOING ALL THE WAY

WHEN IT'S TWO FOR THE ROAD

Not that long ago, in a galaxy too close to forget about, everyone knew how to fall in love. When it was your turn to take romance, the rules were simple—just do what every man did when he encountered Audrey Hepburn. Gregory Peck charmed her in exotic caves, Humphrey Bogart behaved 20 years younger, Albert Finney stalked out of the water like the Creature from the Black Lagoon (where he'd pretended to drown) and demanded a kiss, Rex Harrison lost all composure, Cary Grant plied her with charades, Peter O'Toole stole a million, and Sean Connery rescued and then died for her. What more did you need to know?

Ms. Hepburn is gone now. In her place we have—Lorena Bobbitt, Ricki Lake, Jenny Jones, the woman who composted her husband because he kept turning off the Home Shopping Network before she could use Tootie, the young man who snowplowed his girlfriend because she switched to decaf, Courtney Love, and Demi Moore.

If you fall for the media, the only state more hellish to be in than a relationship right now is Chechnya—and there, at least, you know to sleep with one eye open.

This is not good. This is also not true. There are happy couples, promise, sure as My*T*Fine still makes chocolate pudding that turns you young. Great recipes don't change, no matter what the bill of fare is for the day. Remember the right ingredients, and if every day doesn't start with breakfast at Tiffany's, perhaps one of them may end with your funny face also whispering "I've loved you more than my life." Sounds better than a snowplow to me.

- No one "wins" a quarrel. Settle it.

- Don't do everything and go everywhere together. You'll have nothing to talk about later.

- If you want something so badly, buy it for yourself. Just don't pass it off as a present.

- Don't shop together. Not groceries, not clothes, not furniture. Everyone shops at a different pace. If the purchase concerns a decision that must be made by two, bring the other one along when you've narrowed it down.

- No aspect of love is ever a 50-50 proposition, including economics. If you make more, contribute more, without complaint or comment. Don't you ever use it in an argument.

- Of course, this is obvious, but if you can't remember when you did it last, here's a reminder. Bring home gifts, have special dinners, fill the room with flowers, and unplug the phone for no reason.

♦ With the exception of Mother's Day, when the ramifications are too complex for most advanced clinical psychologists, there is no law, in either Testament or the Constitution, that declares you must visit someone's family over holidays. Besides, aren't you guys a family? Stay home, or go away on your own holiday. Not always (there are wills and trust funds set up for the kids to contend with). But not never.

♦ If you're the slob, don't fight over it. Get a cleaning person. And pay for it, happily.

♦ For the winter, buy flannel sheets.

♦ Don't stop dating each other.

♦ If you're living with Kreskin, fine, say nothing and seethe. If you're not, say, "This bothers me. Can we change it?"

♦ Rinse out the sink after you use it.

♦ Do nothing, together.

♦ Put the seat down.

♦ Be cheerful more than you already are.

- Don't put the television in the bedroom.

- Laugh at everything, unless the face opposite yours tightens, which means what was said was not a joke and you have a nanosecond to pretend you've stepped on something sharp.

- Don't use pet names in public.

- Nothing worth having should ever be attached to a balloon.

- Belittling your partner behind his/her back, even in jest, is lower than a maggot's exercise mat.

- If you think underwear that proclaims HOME OF THE WHOPPER and SPICY WHEN HOT is the ticket, you probably believe that Dow really does great things. When you want to get cute, factor in the difference between sexy and vulgar. There is one.

- In the movies, people break up over big problems. In real life, they break up over paint chips. Have one room, or at least a space, where you make all the decorating decisions.

- Your friends deserve time alone with you.

- You're just a wave, not the water.

- Clip your toenails, often and in private.

- Don't think with your mouth open.

- Remember sometimes the best fish has the most bones.

- Never spend five bucks on a card. Buy a blank one and pick up a pen. Don't try to be D. H. Lawrence. Don't quote anyone else. Write your heart out and maybe you'll finally trust in the adage about good things and small packages.

THINK ON YOUR FEET

AND MAYBE THEY WON'T WIND UP IN YOUR MOUTH

GOOD IDEA: Giving a gift certificate to a health spa
BAD IDEA: Giving a gift certificate to a weight-loss center

GOOD IDEA: Bringing home *Casablanca*, fluffing up the pillows
BAD IDEA: Not pressing PLAY before the end of *NFL Today*

GOOD IDEA: Making reservations at the fency-shmenciest eatery in town
BAD IDEA: Keeping so mum about the surprise she doesn't dress up

GOOD IDEA: A letter
BAD IDEA: A message on the answering machine

GOOD IDEA: Coming home with only champagne and caviar
BAD IDEA: Getting drunk

GOOD IDEA: Always imagining it's your first date
BAD IDEA: Acting like such a geek that she'll believe it is too

GOOD IDEA: Giving expensive chocolates
BAD IDEA: Saying they're your mom's favorites

GOOD IDEA: A picnic
BAD IDEA: Camping

GOOD IDEA: Cleaning the bathroom
BAD IDEA: Acting as if you should be thanked

GOOD IDEA: Offering to help
BAD IDEA: Exclaiming "All you had to do was ask!"

GOOD IDEA: Promising to call before you come over
BAD IDEA: Calling 20 minutes after you were supposed to be
           there

GOOD IDEA: Bringing in the laundry
BAD IDEA: Not picking up the laundry

GOOD IDEA: Unafraid of being romantic
BAD IDEA: Afraid of being sexy

GOOD IDEA: Surprising
BAD IDEA: Assuming

GOOD IDEA: Discovering a secret meeting place
BAD IDEA: Discovering Victoria's Secret

GOOD IDEA: Having sex in the morning
BAD IDEA: Having sex the morning after

GOOD IDEA: Giving a book of poetry
BAD IDEA: Writing nothing inside but "Love, You know who"

GOOD IDEA: Serving breakfast in bed
BAD IDEA: Leaving dishes in a dry sink till dinner

GOOD IDEA: Buying something really sexy
BAD IDEA: Saying "Looks nice" when it's on

GOOD IDEA: Railing against the commercialism and programmed sentiment of Valentine's and Mother's Day
BAD IDEA: Always coming home empty-stomached and -handed

GOOD IDEA: Just calling to say "I love you"
BAD IDEA: Calling collect

WORKING ETHICS

IN CASE THINGS HAPPEN

**WHAT TO START DOING
IMMEDIATELY**

Write it down. Of course you
can remember that. But why
should you have to?

Shine your shoes.

Take off the school ring.

For God's sake, fix your
teeth.

Leave your laptop home on
vacations.

Fill out your expense report
the day you get back.

Stretch every two hours.

Hang your jacket up instead
of slinging it over the back
of a chair.

Dress the way you want to
be treated.

**WHAT TO STOP DOING
IMMEDIATELY**

Forgetting birthdays.

Making that apologetic little
laugh whenever you
disagree.

Buying short-sleeved "dress"
shirts, which make as much
sense as tennis pants.

Taking your suits to be dry-cleaned every time you take them out of a suitcase. (If you can't iron, give them in to be *pressed.*)

Scheduling your day to the second because you're not in charge of timing.

Asking someone else to change the toner.

Waiting for, or scheduling a meeting with, more than two people at one time, unless you have a watch face you love looking at.

Dropping important mail into the building's mail chute.

Talking business on an elevator.

Getting your shirts laundered and then boxed. Are you giving them out as gifts?

Wearing red, white, and blue if you're not in a marching band.

Taking the elevator to go up or down two floors.

Saying "How are you?" to people while you keep on walking.

Talking about how much things have changed instead of changing.

Being afraid of another human being who isn't facing you with a gun.

OTHER STUFF TO HAVE IN YOUR DESK

Five subway tokens.

Vitamin C.

A mini Dopp kit.

A spare set of house keys.

An extra white dress shirt.

A black round-neck pullover.

A zip code map.

A nail buffer.

A needle and thread.

A Zagat guide.

Talcum powder—for fresh tie stains. (Sprinkle heavily. Leave on for as long as possible. Then nail-brush off. Do not use your hands. They're oily.)

The nicest letter any satisfied client ever wrote you.

The dumbest letter any dissatisfied client ever wrote you.

A picture, taken on vacation, of you and someone else looking really ridiculous.

ENTERTAINING THE CLIENT

If it's confidential, don't go where tables are inches apart and there is more waving than behind that window on the *Today* show.

Atmospheric restaurants seduce not only lovers. Wooing is wooing, whatever the pitch.

If you have no pull and Chez Hoo-hah is booked, call back, use another name, and put "Dr." in front of it.

Don't assume the hole in the wall with great jazz takes plastic.

Any seats are *not* better than no seats.

Seats so close you can smell Shaq's cologne! Does your guest even like basketball?

Note that tickets stamped GENERAL ADMISSION don't guarantee seating. You may be standing in the mosh pit.

All venues can tell you over the phone exactly when the main act goes on.

At intermission, talk about anything but work. Think hard.

Better to go somewhere you're treated fabulously than to go somewhere fabulous.

The last thing you say is not "Do we have a deal?" The last thing you say is "Good night."

HOW TO GET IN SO THE CLIENT CAN GET DOWN

Arrive in a rented limousine—and you'll wait till you weep.

Ditch the wing tips.

Stash the beige trench.

Muss your hair.

If you're still suited up, 86 the tie, leave the shirt buttoned.

Don't speak, don't wave, smile small, don't say you know the owner.

Knit hats, big shirts, black jeans, baggy denim, silver, bright solids, fuzzy sweaters, plaid—*da*. Gold, ponytails, bleached denim, stripes, appliqués, running shoes, baseball caps—*nyet*.

Your party all male? Might as well send out for pizza.

Do you own anything in leather that's beat-up? Even a saddle will help.

A FEW NOTES FOR THE BOSS

Never say "I know how you feel."

Never use the phrase "people skills."

Never underestimate a compliment.

Can you say "I don't know" without stuttering?

Don't try to be a buddy. You're not allowed. Be a boss. That's hard enough.

A FEW NOTES FOR THE EMPLOYEE

A promise not notarized only sounds promising.

Don't do it for the compliment.

It's rarely all about you.

Quality is not always job 1.

Blood is thicker than coffee.

Never compare your treatment to someone else's.

Always have a picture of your kid within eyeshot. If no kid, your pet. If you've neither, get either, and then get out the camera.

IT'S TIME TO CHECK THOSE PRIORITIES

When the cleaning woman starts telling you how she really feels.

When you've stopped caring who wins the Oscars.

When you've forgotten to call about the discounted airfares.

When you're known for your ties.

When no charity has sent you a thank-you note in over six months.

When you've stopped smoking—and taken up cigars.

THE ONLY PEOPLE YOU SHOULD BLATANTLY SUCK UP TO

The receptionist.

The UPS guy.

The conductor of the 6:11 express.

Your garage attendant.

The Toys "R" Us salesman who inventories Mighty Morphin Power Rangers.

Anyone who calls from the IRS.

MOVIE QUOTES THAT COULD COME IN HANDY

"Badges! We don't need no stinking badges!"

—*The Treasure of the Sierra Madre*

"What a stunning apartment! Books are so decorative!"

—*Auntie Mame*

"Sometimes you win. Sometimes you lose. Sometimes it rains."

—*Bull Durham*

"Do you think I'd be working in a place like this if I could afford a real snake?"

—*Blade Runner*

"You get what you settle for."

—*Thelma & Louise*

YOU'RE FOOLING YOURSELF IF YOU THINK:

The old one-button suits in the closet are the same as the new ones in the store.

The old two-button suits in the closet are the same as the new ones in the store.

The old three-button suits in the closet are the same as the new ones in the store.

You have to toss these suits out. A good tailor can make them all like the new ones in the store.

A dark shirt and tie make you look like a gangster. You wish.

Strangers in restaurants will drop their cutlery if you change your hairstyle.

A new suit won't make much of a difference.

Home hair dye looks real.

Real men never put their hands on their hips.

Smart folk don't make stupid decisions.

It's not the money, it's the principle.

Another man doesn't clock everything you have on.

YOU MUST REMEMBER THESE

It's a dog-eat-dog world out there. And they're short on napkins.

There are no atheists at an audit.

The only people with the right to yell at you have the same last name as you.

Nobody hears anything else you say when you curse.

"I'm there for you." But with what?

No one's indispensable, except to your bank account.

They don't know what they'd do without you, but they'll think of something if they have to.

How many good sports make the All-Star Team?

The truth hurts, but where?

Age comes in on little crow's-feet.

It's lonely at the top, but you have so much more space.

As long as your family loves you, who cares?

THE BOOKLET OF KNOWLEDGE

YOU KNOW MORE THAN
YOU THINK

YOU KNOW THAT:

**YOU NEED A NEW PIN-
STRIPED SUIT IF:**

Your tailor offers to float
you a loan.

You spray water on it after
ironing to flatten the shine
that's obliterating the
stripes.

Teenagers can't get enough
of those lapels.

The cabbie says you look
"snazzy."

A guest on *Montel Williams*
is wearing the same one.

**YOU'RE THE OLDEST ONE
IN THE ROOM BECAUSE:**

You said you went to the
original Woodstock and
everyone believed you.

You raved about this great
album by Ella and someone
asked, "You mean CD?"

You told them you grew up
near the Polo Grounds and
they wanted to know if you
ever learned how to play.

At this black-tie dinner no
one is complimenting you on
your new cummerbund.

She called him def and you
said you were sorry, you
didn't know.

YOU'VE OVERDRESSED AS SOON AS:

You realize you're the only one in a long-sleeved shirt.

Someone offers to hold your blazer during the sack races.

You enter the "pool party" with your own cue.

The job interviewer notes, "That's a nice suit."

You reveal having chosen between costume and creative black tie, and other guests tell you how much they admire your courage.

YOU'VE BEEN NEGLECTING THINGS WHEN:

The ring around the tub falls under its own weight.

The term "tank top" takes on new meaning.

You say you'll catch up and nobody saves you a seat.

Roaches are dying and you haven't set off a bomb.

You have to separate the whites and the colors by guessing.

You beg to meet her there and then ask what she'll be wearing.

You think everyone else is dressing funny.

YOU'RE WORKING TOO HARD IF:

You've locked yourself out more than once this week.

You blanked on your best friend's phone number.

Your think closing a deal is a Kodak Moment.

You show up for an appointment on the right day, at the right time, in the wrong week.

You've eaten breakfast, lunch, and dinner at your desk.

You couldn't think of anywhere else you'd rather be on your birthday.

You've spoken to your kids three nights in a row by phone without using an MCI number.

You don't want to do it.

You can't do it.

You're not even thinking about it.

THERE'S NO SUCH THING AS:

One size fits all.

Dishwasher safe.

Less fat, more flavor.

Never needs ironing.

Strike that from the record.

Tastes just like chicken.

Making up for lost time.

An attractive pair of brogues.

A hip rep tie.

Being just like family if you're not.

Cheap seats with full view.

Classic fashion.

YOU'RE NOT A SHOPPER, SINCE:

The salesman stopped smiling when you asked to see something like what you have on, but in blue.

You said you didn't have to try it on because "I've always been a 32." The next day they said they gave credit on returns only.

It took more than two minutes to choose a tie, and you didn't buy both.

You asked for the dressing room to put on a turtleneck.

You couldn't believe the sales tax.

THERE'S A BRIDGE TO BROOKLYN WITH YOUR NAME ON IT IF YOU BELIEVE:

"It's *you!*"

NO APPOINTMENT NECESSARY

"They should be ready in eight weeks."

"Drop by anytime."

"We should do this again real soon."

"It's nothing personal."

"Next time, my treat."

YOU CAN STILL HAVE FUN IF:

You leave for vacation with a shoulder bag.

You stumble home after the

sun comes up and don't brag about it.

You start calling people at 6:00, and then have it rolling by 8:00.

The kids don't believe you're their dad.

You're awakened by a "Good morning" that sings.

IT'S TIME TO SAY GOOD NIGHT WHEN:

You talk about finding a way onto the information highway and someone wants to know if it runs anywhere near Ronkonkoma.

The maître d' offers you a tie.

The host starts referring to his wife as "the old ball and chain."

The salesman says you look just great in that four-button double-breasted jacket, and you're 5′ 8″.

Anyone shushes everyone and says, "Oh, I got one! There was this priest, this minister, and this rabbi . . ."

YOU'RE PROBABLY GOING TOO FAST IF YOU START:

Kissing your wife good night on both cheeks.

Dressing the dog.

Thinking you've got to have more than three tuxedoes and you're not in an orchestra.

Considering Friday as part of the weekend.

Finding it harder to make an appointment for a haircut than for an MRI.

Your session by telling the shrink you're down on yourself for missing an art opening.

Wishing they'd open up Central Park to traffic on weekends.

Worrying that your wardrobe has too much color.

YOU'RE RIGHT BECAUSE:

You can afford to be quiet.

They start talking faster.

No one apologizes, but the next day they all say good morning first.

At least three people ask if it's by Armani.

You sleep peacefully, two days later.

SOMETHING'S WRONG WHEN:

The salesman doesn't look at you but at the mirror and goes, "Hmmm."

Your partner gives you a self-help book for Christmas.

Your dinner guest arrives with mums.

You haven't missed a mirror.

Your date looks at the menu and goes, "Oh, look. Shrimp!"

She says "sure" more than once while looking straight ahead, and then adds a "whatever."

You go to sleep like spoons and one of you feels like a salad fork.

YOU'RE IN LOVE WHEN:

You wish the movie you waited two hours on line for was over now.

People you once stared at unrequitedly ask if you're free for lunch.

You sleep straight through the night.

You still think your job stinks, but hey, it's just a job.

The two of you sit in the same room, quietly doing different things, and you don't think anything's wrong. And you're right.

Printed in the United States
by Baker & Taylor Publisher Services